THE STEAMPUNK
USER'S MANUAL

THE STEAMPUNK USER'S MANUAL

AN ILLUSTRATED
PRACTICAL AND WHIMSICAL GUIDE
TO CREATING
RETRO-FUTURIST
DREAMS

**DESIRINA
BOSKOVICH**
AND
**JEFF
VANDERMEER**

ABRAMS IMAGE — NEW YORK

CONTENTS

... INTRODUCTION

WHY STEAMPUNK? 12
BASICS ABOUT THE CREATIVE PROCESS 15
USING THIS BOOK 17

... CHAPTER **1**

STEAMPUNK ART AND MAKING 23

"Old Hat"? Steering Clear of Clichés: Goggles, Gears . . . and Clockwork Insects 34
Pursuing the New: Diversity, Realism, Biotech, and More 38
◉ Finding Inspiration: Tips from Artists and Makers 42
Hands-on Handicraft: The "DIY" Ideal 48
Developing Your Steam-era Skills 60
Meeting Challenges: The Methodical versus "Happy Accidents" 68
Advice for New Artists and Makers 72
Projects:
  ⚙ Creating the Chai Cycle *by James MacIntyre with Toni Green* 30
  ⚙ Making Steampunk Magnets from Used Bottle Caps *by Catherine Cheek* 44
  ⚙ Building a Steam-powered Orrery *by William Francis* 56
  ⚙ Making a Collaged Steampunk Stand-up Greeting *by Ramona Szczerba* 64
  ✴ Thomas Willeford's Steam-powered Mecha-Penguin *by Scott Miller* 74
◉ Dadd, Richard: Fantastic Victoriana *by Jess Nevins* 82

... CHAPTER **2**

STEAMPUNK DESIGN: FASHION, ARCHITECTURE, AND INTERIORS 85

How Retro-futurism Is Influencing Fashion, Architecture, and Interior Design 89
Original Illustration *by Molly Crabapple* 91
◍ Reuse. Reenvision. Repeat: Retro-futurist Fashion *by Katherine Gleason* 92
Three Rings Interior—Because We Can 100
Truth Coffee Shop Interior—Haldane Martin 102
The Future of Steampunk Fashion and Design: In with the Old *and* the New 107
◉ Finding Inspiration: Tips from Designers 114
Steampunk Fashion and Design: A DIY State of Mind 116
School for Steampunks: Mastering Hands-on Skills 118
From Pattern to Product: The Working Process 125
Advice for New Designers 129
✴ Steamarama: The RetroFuture Home of Yesterday and Tomorrow *by Bruce and Melanie Rosenbaum* 130
Project:
  ⚙ Crafting a Rococopunk Jacket from Found Materials *by Megan Maude* 120
◍ Reade House: Fantastic Victoriana *by Jess Nevins* 136

... CHAPTER 3

STEAMPUNK STORYTELLING 139

Finding the Path to Steampunk 143

Steering Clear of Clichés and Pursuing the New 150

⊕ Kraken vs. Airship: Battle Scene *by Richard Preston and Jeremy Zerfoss* 154

The DIY Approach 156

⊕ Objects as Narrative: Jake von Slatt's Fake Machines 158

Original Artwork *by Ivica Stevanovic* 162

Steampunk Collections 164

⊕ Illustrating the Steampunk Story *by Irene Gallo* 166

The Working Process 170

Dealing with Challenges 172

Advice for New Writers 174

✻ Writing Exercises: Repurposing Art *by Matthew Cheney* 176

◈ Detroit Installation: Fantastic Victoriana *by Jess Nevins* 180

... CHAPTER 4

STEAMPUNK MUSIC AND PERFORMANCE 183

Exploration and Adventure: Steampunk's Central Story 187

⊕ Anna Chen's *The Steampunk Opium Wars* 190

Bringing Steampunk to the Stage 192

⊕ "Building a Utopian Playland": Steampunk and Performance *by Diana M. Pho* 196

Finding the Path to Steampunk 200

Steampunk Music's Past and Future: Steering Clear of Clichés 202 Pursuing the New 204

DIY for Musicians and Performers 205

◉ Finding Inspiration: Tips from Musicians and Performers 206

⊕ The Art of Found-Percussion *by Eric Farber* 208

Learning the Basics: The Steampunk Musician's Tools 218

The Creative Life: A Working Process for Musicians and Performers 220

Collaboration with the Band 222

Collaboration with the Audience 224

⊕ Reproduction and Adaptation: A Steampunk Story from Page to Performance *by Nancy Hightower* 226

Advice for Aspiring Musicians and Performers 230

Project: 🛠 Making a Bonebox and Canjo *by Matt Lorenz* 212

... CHAPTER 5

RETRO-FUTURE FANTASIES AND STEAMPUNK DREAMS 233

Big Ideas from Artists and Makers 234

. . . from Designers and Fashionistas 240

. . . from Storytellers 242

. . . from Musicians and Performers 245

... ABOUT THE AUTHORS 250

... ACKNOWLEDGMENTS 251

... ILLUSTRATION AND PHOTO CREDITS 252

... INDEX 253

VAN OIJEN 2013

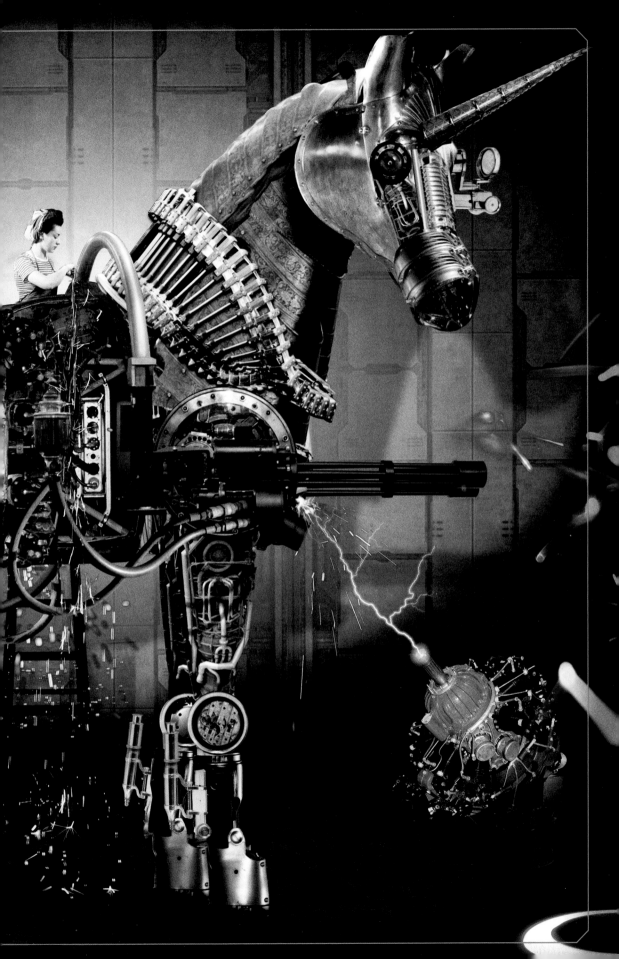

WHY STEAMPUNK?

Both cultural theorists and at-home Steampunkers have dedicated plenty of time to exploring the appeal of the Industrial Age aesthetic for artists, makers, and laypeople alike. There are many reasons that people are drawn to retro-futurism, but one that particularly stands out is the variety and contrast it offers to the prevailing styles of recent decades. "For the last thirty or so years," artist and maker Herr Döktor comments, "design has been a form of reductionism: computers in plain beige/gray/black boxes, streamlining making cars and other vehicles indistinguishable, and so forth. Steampunk (and its ilk) has allowed some to take a new look at the world around us, with an eye to both the past and the future."

PAGES 2–3
"Victorian Robo Detective and Dr. WATTson" by Guy Himber
PAGE 4
"Exorcist" by James Ng
PAGE 7
Prague (Praha) by Sam Van Olffen
PAGES 8–9
Artist and maker Thomas Willeford's studio
PAGES 10–11
The Great Mechanical Unicorn by Sam Van Olffen
OPPOSITE
Steampunk musician Andrew O'Neill of The Men That Will Not Be Blamed For Nothing. Photo by Ria Osborne. Frame by John Coulthart.

Ramona Szczerba, a psychologist and artist known for her watercolor and collage pieces, agrees. "In terms of design, I think it's a great balance to ever-more-sleek modernism. While cars and phones and televisions are all becoming impregnable smooth pods that stay inert until you touch them, Steampunk designs favor visible workings and surface ornamentation. . . . Plus, if it breaks, you stand a chance of fixing it yourself without voiding the manufacturer's warranty!"

Szczerba also notes Steampunk's flexibility as a tool for the imagination: "As a psychologist, I suspect that Steampunk is a doorway to creativity and imagination in the same way we consider the Rorschach to be a way to access the unconscious. We are all looking at the same blot, but the interest comes from each individual and what of herself she imposes upon and brings to it."

One thing is certain: Steampunk and the whole of the retro-futuristic aesthetic offer a much broader playground for a creative person, a buffet of intriguing approaches and fresh looks to set one's work apart from the competition. For the working creator, the flexibility of a bigger toolbox may be exceedingly helpful in the day-to-day. "As a designer, I think and make in terms of appropriateness for the design strategy and message needs; certain projects call for certain visual aesthetic directions," says Danny Warner. (His pioneering work with motion posters is a concrete example of this principle.) Warner adds, "My first Steampunk-inspired work was in the realm of display typography. I used schemata and other iconography of simple machinery to develop new ideas in typographic form."

Doktor A is another popular maker and artist of the Steampunk world. His work runs the gamut from zany toys to whimsical sculptures to 2-D art and illustration, and he is particularly known for his Mechtorian series — steam-powered toys that double as the wacky citizens of a fictional world called Retropolis. Doktor A agrees that the lush looks of retro-futurism are a welcome and refreshing change. "I think it's nice to see people enjoying embellishment again," he says. "I feel that as technology in particular becomes ever more powerful and ever more integrated into our lives that we should not expect it all to be presented in only one style. I think it's important that people make it work for them in a way that they are comfortable interacting with, and in a style of their choosing, whatever that may be."

In many ways, Steampunk is the visual vernacular that defines the current era: both our fascination with technology and progress, and our nostalgic longing for a simpler age. Slowly, the aesthetic has slipped into our films, our graphic novels, our fashion, our interior decor, and even our digital lives. "Retro-futurism, specifically its blend of midcentury modernism and art deco, has heavily influenced everything from skeuomorphic touch-screen interfaces to modern movies," says Mark Givens, an art and culture scholar and editor in chief of *MungBeing Magazine*.

Givens also feels that Steampunk is even more deeply tied into the cultural zeitgeist, saying, "[Steampunk] has greatly influenced the look and style of the early twenty-first-century youth movement—the hipsters—with its handlebar mustaches, brass, and muted colors."

And now, these hipsters, yuppies, and penny-pinchers alike are developing passions that would make their grandparents proud; they're mastering forgotten skills and returning to the land, practicing hobbies such as gardening, sewing, canning, quilting, woodworking; even making their own cheese, curing their own meats, and brewing their own beer. The desire to tinker with our machines and create something both functional and beautiful stems from the same core impulse.

The best thing about Steampunk, however, is its big-tent mentality. As Givens says, there is room for "makers and tinkers, DIY and craft assemblages, and anachronistic bike riders." Not to mention, a growing global movement of Steampunkers across the world, who are reinventing the looks of retro-futurism with respect to their own unique cultural contexts.

Still not sure? Well, you'll discover many more answers to that question in the chapters to follow.

BASICS ABOUT THE CREATIVE PROCESS

At some level, each and every artistic project is unique, with its own problems to solve and its own path from conception to completion—especially if you are the kind of maker who always wants a fresh challenge, a bigger puzzle to solve. That said, there are a few basic steps that usually go into executing a creative project.

Step 1: INSPIRATION. The first step, of course, is getting an idea; this idea frequently emerges as a random burst of inspiration. Other times, the idea evolves as the result of a conscious decision to sit down and brainstorm.

"I pace and think. Or, if sitting in a task chair, I rock and think. This is most of the work. A smaller proportion of the work is actually spending all the labor on the creation of the art itself."

—*Keith Thompson*

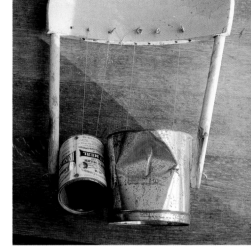

Step 2: DEVELOPMENT. Usually, an artist or maker will sketch out their idea with preliminary drawings, simple sketches, and some element of text.

"I get inspired, take a lot of notes, and make sketches. I try to wireframe larger projects and whittle them down into stages on paper or in my phone."

—*Libby Bulloff*

ABOVE
Chair back with cans, a **DIY** musical instrument by Matt Lorenz.
BELOW
La Tetera de Hobart (Hobart's Kettle) by Oscar Sanmartin

Step 3: EXECUTION. This is where the creator goes to their workshop—
even if that workshop is just the kitchen table—and begins to build. Or
draw. Or paint. Or cut. Or saw. Or weld. Or whatever the project requires.

"Depending on constraints such as budget, time, and facilities, you
either sit down at the drawing board and create some concepts or you just
sit down at the workbench and start playing around with bits. (I have boxes
full of random 'bits' just waiting to be built into something or other.) Budget
is generally the driving force, though—sometimes you have the luxury of
a complete design process and can tool specific pieces, other times you just
have to stick lots of pieces together and make it up as you go along."

—*Mark Cordory*

Step 4: REVISION AND COMPLETION. Sometimes it's helpful to
take a break and come back to the work with fresh eyes. Maybe it's done—

or maybe it needs a bit more work. In a few cases, it may even be time to go back to the literal or figurative drawing board: Step 2. But that's how the process of creation works.

"Research and organization. Shaping the problem. Brainstorming, and generation of possibilities and prototypes. Testing, getting feedback, honing. Then committing to a direction, and executing it. Then—and this is important—coming back later (once I hopefully have some distance and a more dispassionate perspective on the project), and evaluating where it succeeds and doesn't, to learn for next time."   —*Danny Warner*

Sometimes it can be hard to start a project, but if you take the leap, incredible things can happen. More important, the journey you undertake when you engage your imagination is often as satisfying as reaching the finish line.

USING THIS BOOK

The Steampunk User's Manual is designed to help you dream both big and small, showcasing both small-scale, practical projects and pie-in-the-sky "big ideas," to show you the range that's possible. Some of these projects are so whimsical you might not be able to do them at all—but that's okay. One person's unmakeable one-hundred-foot-high Steampunk penguin is another's plot device for a sprawling Steampunk novel trilogy.

While each chapter varies from subject to subject, delving into territories most relevant to the medium at hand, there are a few sections you can expect to see with regularity throughout this book.

Past and Future: Steering Clear of Clichés

In this section, we take a look at the state of the art in Steampunk, with our interviewees weighing in. We point out a few conventions that are now so prevalent they've become cliché (we're sure you can name a few), and more important, we take a long look forward, exploring the fresh and innovative ideas that may define Steampunk's future.

Finding Inspiration: Where Do You Get Your Ideas?

Everyone can use a bit more inspiration at times, but the process of inspiration is a tricky one to pin down. For this section, we asked artists, makers, designers, storytellers, musicians, and performers where they find their best and most innovative ideas. Their answers are inspiring in and of themselves—and a fantastic reminder that ideas really can be anywhere and everywhere you look.

DIY: Practical Applications for Your Field

What does DIY mean for an interior designer? A storyteller? A musician? This section is jam-packed with personal insight from working professionals and passionate hobbyists alike on what DIY means to them, both as a guiding ethos for their work and as a hands-on aspect of their daily practice.

ABOVE
Image from Steampunk
Haunted House, created by
Zach Morris and Third Rail
Projects. Photo by Chad
Heird.

OPPOSITE
Detail of Serpent Twins,
created by Jon Sarriugarte
and Kyrsten Mate, and their
"Empire of Dirt" crew. Design
team Because We Can as-
sisted in the fabrication and
provided additional support.

OVERLEAF
Peace Treaty by Keith Thompson, an interior illustration
from *The Manual of Aero-
nautics: An Illustrated Guide
to the Leviathan Series* by
Scott Westerfeld. Reprinted
with the permission of Simon
Pulse, an imprint of Simon &
Schuster Children's Publishing Division.

Back to the Basics: Developing Your Skills

If you want to DIY, you never stop learning. (Which, since you're reading a book called *The Steampunk User's Manual*, you probably already know!) This section contains tips and advice on expanding your tool set and honing your skills.

The Working Process

Our creative experts offer inside looks into their own working methods, whether those take place at the drafting table, the word processor, or the recording studio. Examples abound, as there is no one-size-fits-all when it comes to creative work! With their insight, we chart the creative process from brainstorming session to finished product.

Seven Pieces of Advice

In this section, you'll find valuable words to take to the road; succinct summations from our creative experts on the values and practices that enable their success. You can scribble these nuggets of wisdom on a note card to tape over your desk, or simply browse and be inspired. The aim is to take everything you've learned in each chapter and turn it into practical insight for the creative journey to come.

Rather than tell you what you should and shouldn't do, we've let the words of some very talented creators show what has worked for them, with copious quotes that provide insight into the creative process on both a nuts-and-bolts level and the level of idea and inspiration.

It's your job to take what you find here and apply it on your own, picking and choosing what works best for your own personal passions and skill set. We hope you have fun, and we hope this book helps spark your imagination. We're looking forward to your own stories of creation.

— Desirina Boskovich and Jeff VanderMeer, January 2014

LES UTOPIES DE LA NAVIGATION
AÉRIENNE AU SIÈCLE DERNIER.

COLLECTION 476   2ème Série (N° 2)   ROMANET & Cie IMP EDIT. PARIS.

CHAPTER
1

STEAMPUNK ART AND MAKING

The Steampunk aesthetic has seized the imagination of artists, designers, and craftspeople of all kinds. At the heart of this enthusiasm is a dedication to both good old-fashioned handicraft and bold new ways of thinking. Steampunk revels in futures that never were, and the past as it might have been. This bounty of alternate ways of thinking about the world offers plenty of space to evolve—and lots of room to play. To create in a Steampunk mode means giving careful thought to how to personalize retro-futurism.

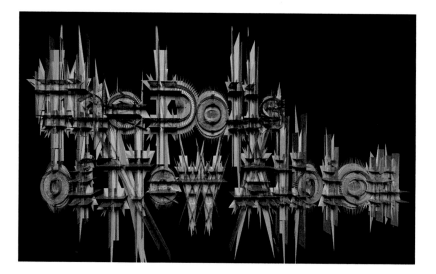

PAGE 22
Utopian Flying Machines of the Previous Century, from a series of chromolithograph prints published in Paris between 1890 and 1900. Exhibited in 2003–4 by the Library of Congress for the show *The Dream of Flight*.

ABOVE
Still from a motion poster by Danny Warner

OPPOSITE
Lilies on Stage by Doktor A

Steampunk can be brassy or demure. It can be kitschy, gothic, surreal, and whimsical by turns—and despite the clichés, Steampunk's palette, as exemplified by its art, roves far beyond the simple sepia tones of a washed-out Western—from black-and-white minimalism to jewel-toned kaleidoscope extravaganzas.

Take, for example, the retro-futuristic work of Danny Warner, a designer who is pioneering the avant-garde motion poster, a hybrid form that combines animation and design. (You may have previously seen a motion poster at a mall or an airport, where they sometimes display information or advertisements to fast-moving passersby.) Warner's motion poster for the Steampunk opera *The Dolls of New Albion* "consists of biomechanical nanoputia churning inside one of the character's heads, with Steampunk-inspired animated typography and a beautiful slice of the opera's score for the sound. It's very minimalist, and inspired by the fusion of biological and mechanical." The high-resolution poster is locally displayed on a vertical high-definition screen.

Minimalist? Perhaps, and yet the poster also showcases the essential paradox of Steampunk: Sometimes even "minimalist" can mean complex. It also showcases the wonderful way in which Steampunk can reframe the question "What is functional and what is decorative?"

But true minimalism is also possible. Libby Bulloff—one of the Steampunk community's beloved pioneers—approaches her current work using vintage techniques to cast an antique lens (often literally) on contemporary subjects and settings. Bulloff's love of the retro-futuristic aesthetic led her to obsessively study wet-plate collodion photography, an early method of photographic processing that dates back to the 1850s, when it began replacing the daguerreotype. Bulloff and her partner, Stephen Robinson, now have a tintype studio where they shoot old-fashioned portraiture and still

lifes. "There's a visceral quality to black-and-white photos with scratches and flaws that perfect, multi-megapixel digital images can't naturally have," says Bulloff. "Each tintype Stephen and I pour is completely unique and unpredictable. There are no copies."

Whereas Bulloff has been moving toward a sparser palette and approach, Brian Kesinger, of Otto and Victoria fame, demonstrates what's possible to accomplish with vibrant colors. And not just color—in *Green Tea*, from his Tea Girls series, Kesinger also plays with medium, by tinting ink with actual green tea, and then using watercolor to heighten the colors.

Kesinger gets even more experimental with color in his Otto and Victoria series, and not only because its heroine is a teal-coiffed beauty, although her hair does set the tone for most of the illustrations. In *Hiding*, Victoria looks for her cephalopod suitor, Otto, who has used his camouflaging abilities to blend in with his surroundings, creating a visual effect that tricks the viewer as well as Victoria. Our eyes are drawn to her teal hair, punctuated by teal ribbons. But Otto has nestled into the most colorful area of the canvas, blending in with the mauve-striped wallpaper, the green rug, the raw

ABOVE
Hiding by Brian Kesinger
OPPOSITE ABOVE
Von Slatt Steampunker by
Mike Pecci
OPPOSITE LEFT
Steampunk bus, photo by
Jake von Slatt

sienna of the bookshelf. Eventually, these colorful trails lead us to discover the various guises of Otto's eight arms.

Driving a bus through all of this—literally—is maker Jake von Slatt, founder of the Steampunk Workshop, whose aesthetic combines both the practical and the decorative, especially on one of his largest palettes, his Steampunk bus. In such creations, you can see the large-scale application of many different approaches to art and making—not just in the way von Slatt, as a tinker, uses throwaway bits of machinery for his creations, but in how he furnishes them. The "punk" in Steampunk is on display, but the impulse toward the beautiful isn't abandoned.

Von Slatt points out that, "For many years, technology-based hobbies, such as electronics and amateur radio, have been in decline. The magazines that supported [these endeavors] are all either out of business or now purely gadget review rags—and there used to be dozens of them. Many towns had stores packed with kits and components [from] national companies . . . build-it-yourself versions of radios, electric eyes, amplifiers, and even color television sets."

Because technological hobbies now "lack such defined paths," von Slatt believes that the current rise in their popularity means that "young people are developing these hobbies later, and infusing them with what they are already passionate about. This is what's leading to the development of fascinating hybrids like Steampunk."

In von Slatt's work, the confluence of art and science is most apparent, because he has an eye for repurposing what other people term "junk," not just with a tinker's eye, but with the eye of someone who understands why one abandoned light fixture is more aesthetically pleasing than another. In a field where repurposing is prevalent, that is a priceless gift for any creator.

Creating the Chai Cycle

by James MacIntyre with Toni Green

After my first experience of Burning Man, I wanted to make an art bike of my own for the next year, and I really wanted it to be customized for everything I need while riding through the desert all day and night. I wanted something that suited me and would be easy to spot in a crowd of other parked rides.

From there, I considered ideas for either building a bike-and-sidecar combo or something with a modified trike. It all depended on what materials I found that worked, or that found me. I complimented someone on his vintage cargo trike, and it turned out that he is a bike mechanic who had a second vintage trike that he was willing to sell. The trike that found me is a 1970s Pashley Picador from the UK.

I'm a chef by trade and passion, so I thought it was natural to want to be able to nourish people at various art events and random encounters. I didn't want to deal with the logistics of serving food, so I was drawn to the idea of a good cup of chai tea to warm the body and soul during the chilly desert sunrises.

My ideal was basically a large double-walled Kelly Kettle, which has a fire chamber and another space to brew the tea. I looked at different ways to modify something to suit my needs or to build from scratch, but was lucky to find a fully ornate Turkish brass samovar set in a thrift store.

THIS SPREAD AND OVERLEAF SPREAD
Detailed shots of the Chai Cycle, with James MacIntyre, taken at Burning Man. Photos by Nathan Sorochan.

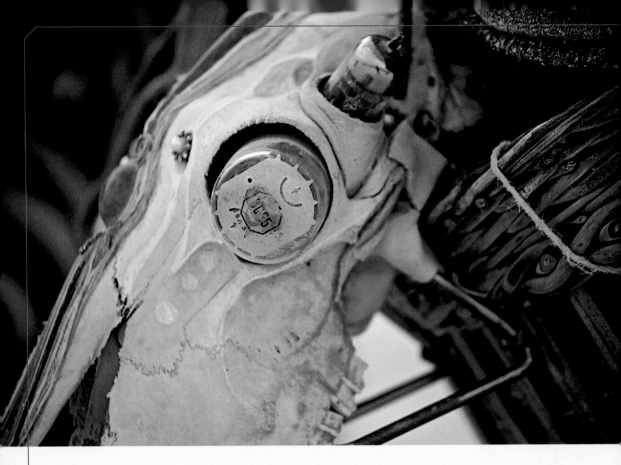

Most of the wood used in the project came from recycling a pallet, plus plywood that was previously a FREE sign at the end of someone's driveway.

The storage trunk on the back of the bike is an old sewing machine box that fit perfectly, so Toni made it funky.

The goat skull on the front basket was originally from a desert in Nevada, but was found at a yard sale before Toni decorated it and added vacuum tubes sourced from someone who used to work for CBC Television. The tubes were originally for black-and-white cameras. Rewired flashlights were embedded in the skull to create the "Wandering Goat headlights." We used recycled metal cowbells from India for the taillights.

When we were fixing up the Chai Cycle for the Steampunk convention at the Empress Hotel, it completely took over our living room. We don't have a proper workshop (just a small art room), so we had to get rid of our couch to accommodate the Chai Cycle in our house. It was insane. We had two months, while working full-time jobs, to make it look super-fancy and polished. When things got snagged, we found that stepping away and working on another part of the project, or on something else for a while, helped.

Every step started with an idea and an overall look and feel to maintain. We adapted and collaborated on everything as we figured it out: what went where, what worked, and what needed to change. It's still a work in progress.

"Old Hat"? Steering Clear of Clichés: Goggles, Gears . . . and Clockwork Insects

Taking the old and making it new might be the point of Steampunk, but while some things are delightfully antiqued, others are just old hat. How do you figure out what's innovatively old? Paying attention to what's been done to death is important, especially for a culture that's only been self-defined as such since about 2007: The rate of change can be oddly explosive for an aesthetic that's looking to the past for inspiration.

Here's a clue: If you're looking at these pages through special retro goggles while holding a gear, you might be buying into Steampunk clichés. The now ubiquitous goggles and gears have practically come to single-handedly define the Steampunk aesthetic.

Artist James Ng gets to the heart of the matter: "There are a few things that spring to mind right away when thinking of Steampunk. Airships, goggles, gears, top hats, and corsets." Goggles and gears are Steampunk's calling cards, its signature moves. In short, they're the visual signal that tells us we are in the wild, magical West of zeppelins and steam. In a sense, they're also a not-so-secret code telling others, "I'm one of you."

So, given their importance, is it time to retire these beloved symbols? Maybe, maybe not. Perhaps it's all a matter of context.

Although Ng points out their ubiquity, he also says, "I wouldn't call them cliché, because they were things that were relevant to the era the original Steampunk culture is based on." But there should still be limits to their use. "One thing that bothers me with Steampunk work is when people simply stick random gears on things and call it a 'Steampunk version.' There has to be some sort of function or concept behind it for that label to be appropriate, because Steampunk is not just decoration." As Herr Döktor adds, "I love gears, as they are both functional and beautiful as a design element."

Further complicating things is the need for storytelling in Steampunk. Usually, the art and making come with fairly elaborate tales behind them, perhaps because the origins of Steampunk are largely literary. Sometimes this idea of "functionality" speaks less to a need for something to actually work than to a need for believable storytelling—that both the creator and the person who enjoys the creation want the tale being told to make sense at the level of the look and feel.

Mark Cordory is a designer and maker whose impressive portfolio includes work for theater, film, and television, as well as artistic exhibitions. He even served for two years as head of props fabrication for the popular television show *Doctor Who*. So he has quite a bit of experience creating visual set pieces and physical objects that are fresh, fascinating, and compelling. Cordory comments, "I like to see *function* in things. . . . To me, Steampunk is about invention and function—that wonderful Victorian drive that brought about the Industrial Revolution—and so I'm always

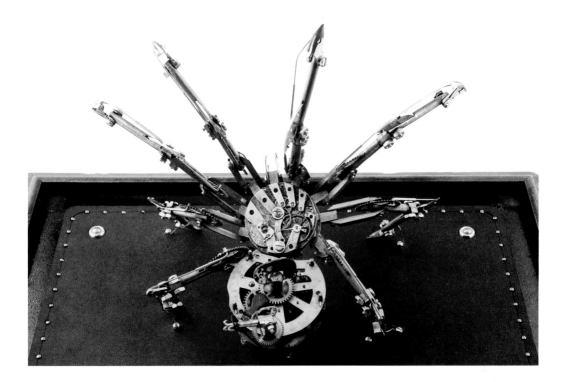

happy when it actually looks like a creation has a purpose and has been put together in a way that looks as though it could conceivably work."

"The best way to avoid what I call the 'cog on a stick' effect," says Thomas Willeford, founder of Brute Force Studios and author of the book *The Steampunk Adventurer's Guide*, "is for things to at least look like they function. You are allowed to do anything you like, but put in the effort."

In addition to putting in the effort, a wider context may also be key. Bulloff's perspective on cliché is that some Steampunkers need to take a second look at the values they promote through their work. "I have grown quite tired of all the pretend weaponry and implied violence in so many Steampunk images," she says. "It is not attractive nor particularly clever to parade about in front of a camera with a plastic gun, especially in the wake of the school shootings in the United States. . . . I would hope that we'd be self-aware enough to realize how crass it is to laud violent imagery or pictures that aren't particularly feminist or intelligent."

This is an especially essential conversation in Steampunk, as much of the artistry and craftsmanship harks back to a Victorian era with attitudes very different from our contemporary ones. The art we create in this vein can either question and challenge those outmoded ways of thinking, or uphold and promote them—sometimes totally apart from the artist's intention.

In brief: Visual shorthands such as goggles and gears can be used to great effect, and you can have great fun creating just about anything in a retro-futuristic style, but look for a fresh twist you can bring to your creations. Even beautiful clockwork insects, as pioneered by creators like Mike Libby, can become too usual through the effect of sheer factory-like repetition. There are now so many riffs on the work of the original artists exploring this area that it may become the next widely recognized cliché in Steampunk.

The Telectroscope was a retro-futuristic art installation by contemporary artist Paul St George, exhibited in London and New York City in 2008. This interactive video project linked enthusiastic audiences from city to city, bringing them face to face in real time as they stood in front of the glass on either side of the "tunnel's" end-points. According to the fictional narrative accompanying the installation, this transatlantic tunnel was devised by St George's great-grandfather, (the mythical) Alexander Stanhope St George. Reportedly, the tunnel burst from the pier heralded by the business end of a six-foot drill bit.

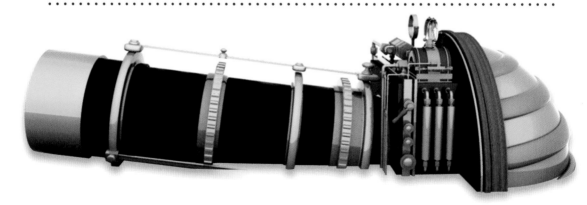

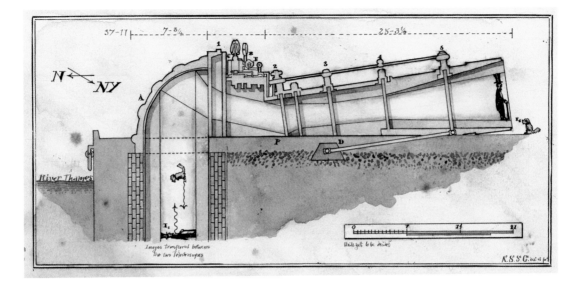

OPPOSITE ABOVE
Telectroscope (installation view at Tower Bridge) by Paul St George. Photo by Matthew Andrews.

OPPOSITE BELOW
London–New York Telectroscope (profile) by Paul St George

ABOVE
Patent drawing for Telectroscope by Paul St George and Felix Bennett

LEFT
Auger drill bit that introduced the Telectroscope by Paul St George. Photo by Matthew Andrews.

Pursuing the New: Diversity, Realism, Biotech, and More

Bringing the "new" into Steampunk art and making can be a source of contention within the community itself. For example, there are those who believe that "Steampunk" must always reference the Industrial Revolution or fictional works thereof, as it played out in England and the United States, and, sometimes, Japan.

But what about other periods of technological change that could be fertile ground for invention? For example, the Islamic Renaissance of the eleventh century resulted in the creation of machines that aren't so different from what we're familiar with from the Industrial Revolution. The ancient Egyptians purportedly had sliding doors that worked in part through use of steam technology.

So is it a particular time and place that Steampunk celebrates and draws inspiration from, or is it instead "like seeking like" across the ages? For a lot of Steampunk now entering the culture, the answer is weighted toward

the limitless bounty of expansion—expanding to allow what is essentially make-believe sometimes grounded in science to find its fullest and most personal expression.

Opening up Steampunk in this way makes for a more diverse community as well: It makes the movement global and opens a thousand new doors, considerably expanding both the story and the aesthetic possibilities.

"I'd love to see more multicultural Steampunk," James Ng says. "I really like the original Victorian-era Steampunk, it has a feel that can't really be replaced or replicated, but I think we can come up with some very fresh imagery if we look for inspiration from different cultures. I don't mean just a person in a Japanese kimono wearing goggles, I mean what that specific culture values, what is important to them, and how they would use the concept of Steampunk to create something new and unique to their culture." At times, the thought experiments can be quite mind-bending; we delve into the underpinnings and pivot points of our history (and all its alternate versions).

ABOVE
Mollusc Tree by Keith Thompson

Even within the traditional setting of Victorian England that characterizes much of today's Steampunk, there is a lot more room for historical accuracy, which in turn would bring something fresh to art and making.

Keith Thompson, perhaps best known for his work on the Leviathan series, creates darkly fanciful illustrations that form intricate and atmospheric windows into other worlds. Still, when it comes to depictions of alternate histories on earth, he'd appreciate greater rigor in the historicity department. "I'd like to see more of an immersion into the mind-set and aesthetics that match the time settings that Steampunk takes its cues from. I'd like to see more art composed in a noncinematographic manner, [reflecting] stories and characters that have mind-sets and motives that exist in their own setting and circumstances, not ours, the observers."

Jake von Slatt points out, "A young woman [during Victorian times] watching a train pull away from the platform could identify all of the parts that made the engine run. The boiler, the firebox, the great steam piston rod that drove the wheels, and the smaller rod that worked the valve gear; these components were all visible, and their functions obvious." Shouldn't even creators working on a small scale with elements of technology need to be able to do the same?

On the other hand, while some want a more historically accurate version of Steampunk, others are interested in a more heavily science-fictional take. Beyond just in novels and short stories, Danny Warner, for example, "would love to see Steampunk grapple more with biotechnological futures

Let us honour the **Kings of The Surface**

For we welcome all guests in their radiant glory and truly our greatest hope is that their visit lasts for the ages.

and nanotechnologies. *Minority Report* stuff. *Gattaca* stuff. *Blade Runner* stuff."

In the first issue of the hugely influential *Steampunk Magazine*, the Catastrophone Orchestra and Arts Collective envisioned the art of Steampunk machines in a similar way: "real, breathing, coughing, struggling, and rumbling parts of the world. They are not the airy intellectual fairies of algorithmic mathematics, but the hulking manifestations of muscle and mind, the progeny of sweat, blood, tears, and delusions. The technology of Steampunk is natural: It moves, lives, ages, and even dies." Their description evokes visions of a whole new take on biotech, with a vast new horizon for a more sci-fi-focused Steampunk to explore.

Perhaps in the near future, retro-futurism will spawn two new subgenres—a more fantastic subgenre with zombies, vampires, and clockwork magic, and a more science-fictional subgenre with biotech, nanotech, and data pirates.

But whatever the future holds, the point is that there is a future for Steampunk art and making—one where it becomes enriched and deepened by exciting ideas that push beyond conventional definitions while still holding true to retro-futurism's core idea.

FINDING INSPIRATION

Tips from Artists *and* Makers

TOP
Clock by Annliz Bonin
BOTTOM
Shutterburg by Doktor A
OPPOSITE
The Stuckists Punk Victorian
by Paul Harvey

"Everything inspires me! The small details of daily life, the books I read, the picture I discover while surfing the net. IDEAS come to me unexpectedly at **odd times**, whether it's when I'm crossing the street, or doing the dishes, or dining with friends."

—*Annliz Bonin*

"I'm inspired by the littlest notions: a nicely plated meal, an old photographic lamp in an antique shop, a pair of pointy shoes. THINGS I don't understand or *that get under my skin* are just as inspiring as things of *obvious beauty*. Some of my best work has resulted from awkward situations or oddball concepts."

—*Libby Bulloff*

"I just have lots of *characters in my head* waiting to get out. Every day, I can potentially see something or visit somewhere that will inspire new characters. I have not yet mined this seam dry. So until I do, I have this urge to keep bringing these beings out of my head and releasing them into the world."

—*Doktor A*

"INSPIRATION can come from a *myriad* of sources: sometimes an image, sometimes suggested by a shape or by looking at an object from an *angle*."

—*Herr Döktor*

"When I start a new project, often I do not have a clear scenario. I find something in my **mind** and I try to bring it to **life**. I do not repeat the form of somebody's inner world, but I dig and search my own brain. All the themes, ideas in my works are usually around us—you just have to see and 'read' them. It is important to value what you see; the world around us is very interesting, but often we are too busy to value it or to guess its secret meanings."

—*Andrey Drozdov*

"I'm *obsessed* by APOLLO, as I like the combination of old and new technologies, with an element of SCIENCE FICTION thrown in. Looking back on the moon landing now and watching the old footage, it seems as much a triumph for Victorian thinking as a 1960s achievement. It had a big effect on me as a child and still does. I recently bought a model of the Saturn V rocket that I was going to build and incorporate with art nouveau decorative elements, but I haven't gotten round to it yet."

—*Paul Harvey*

"My work is rather narrative, telling a story in one or two panels (this depends if the box has a lid or not). Sometimes actual STORIES will INSPIRE my ideas, such as the story of the **Cottingley Fairies**."
—*Louise Kiner*

"The more you are interested by other fields of knowledge, the more you will feed your creativity. . . . Literature, paintings, architecture, absolutely everything. As Jacques Brel said perfectly: 'When you read Rimbaud the evening before, you are richest the day after, but you realize that you wrote much less than you thought.' All my philosophy is in this quote, because I feel richer after seeing skies in a painting of Philippe Jacques de Loutherbourg than I did before. . . . It's with the capacity to always BE SURPRISED that I feed my art."
—*Sam Van Olffen*

"I try to IMAGINE what it must have been like to see the *first television* picture, see the *first film*, or read the *first telegram*. I then try to create an analogous experience that will give a contemporary audience that same thrill and joy."
—*Paul St George*

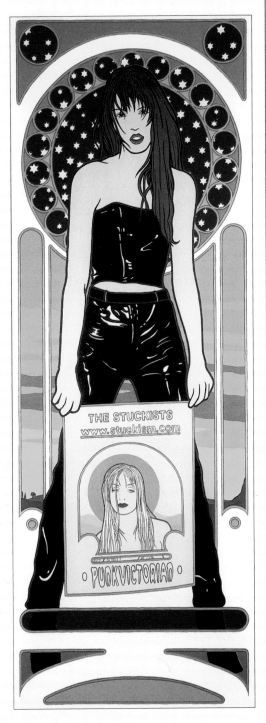

"The images themselves inspire everything. It's like a puzzle I'm putting together. I almost never set out to create a collage depicting a guy and some robots. Rather, I come across an etching of a vintage espresso machine and it looks like a robot to me, so I add bits to it and then it's definitely a robot, and I have a photo of a beautiful guy, but I hate his suit, so he gets a different one and, of course, with an espresso robot, he's going to have a vintage coffee grinder for a hat, and only a giant spoon would do as a walking stick. . . . So I'm off and running. MOTIVATION is something I need to get myself to *exercise* or *clean* out my closet, not to make art. The stories I write for the pieces can be hard. That feels a little bit more like work to me."
—*Ramona Szczerba*

"Science. Film. Product design. Fashion. Architecture. . . . *For me,* **ideas are like happiness.** If you try to look at it, focus directly on it, you can't grab it; it's something that comes along out of the corner of your eye when you're doing what you're supposed to."
—*Danny Warner*

Making Steampunk Magnets from Used Bottle Caps

by Catherine Cheek

In the future, archaeologists may mark bottle caps as the quintessential relic of the twentieth and twenty-first centuries. Ubiquitous and functional, they nevertheless have a comfortable tactile quality, which is perhaps the reason why people have a tendency to hoard them. But what to do with these single-use pieces of metal? With this project, you can upcycle these dregs of modern society into miniature pieces of functional art. You'll need resin, epoxy, bottle caps, art paper, razors (or hairpins), brads (brass fasteners), and small metal cogs. (The cogs used in this example are from the Tim Holtz studio, available at most craft stores.) Because of the cure times of resin and epoxy, this project will take two days to complete.

Take some empty bottle caps and cut out one-inch circles of decorative paper. You can buy this paper at craft stores, or cut up old newspapers, note cards, or whatever else tickles your fancy. Haven't got any bottle caps? Drink, man! Drink! Glue the circles to the bottom of the caps with any sort of glue. I used Elmer's white glue.

Shown opposite are the gears and items I will put into the bottle caps, as well as some blades to use as supports. For those of gentle disposition, one need not use blades. One can use anything small, light, and nonporous that will not bend easily, such as a hairpin. One can purchase most of these gears and the brads (you may know these as brass fasteners or split pins) used as axles at a craft store. Otherwise, you can dismantle a clock (preferably one belonging to someone you dislike).

Dry fit all your pieces so you can be sure they fit. You may need to trim the ends off your brads so they don't quite touch the bottom of the cap.

You'll need a two-part, clear-casting epoxy. Mine is by EasyCast, and for this project, you don't need much. Sixty milliliters of resin will fill approximately fourteen bottle caps. You'll also need some disposable plastic cups, clean stirring sticks, and an accurate (preferably disposable) graduated measuring cup. You can use the plastic measuring cup that comes with cough syrup. VERY IMPORTANT: Follow the directions that come with the resin exactly, down to the letter, even though they may seem fussy and peculiar. If you don't, your resin will not cure, and you will have a sticky morass that must be discarded, along with all the delightful cogs unfortunate enough to have been trapped in it.

fig 1
pour resin

brad

cog

fig 2
stack pieces

supports

partially
filled
cup

Mix the resin carefully. Place the bottle caps on a level surface, and pour the resin until it reaches just below the top of the bottle cap. The next part takes a deft hand. Carefully lay the supports (razors or hairpins) across the top of the bottle cap. Rest your gears on top of these, and use the tiny brad as an axle, lining up the holes on both gears.

I like to use a two-part, five-minute epoxy to glue on the magnets. You don't need a clamp, as the magnets will adhere themselves while the epoxy cures. Do keep them away from one another during the curing time, as magnets prefer the company of their own kind excessively.

Once the epoxy is cured, you should be able to slip out your razors and pins and other rests without trouble. One might find it wise to use pliers. Because the top gears aren't mired in the resin, they should spin freely.

....

Catherine Cheek has published novels, short fiction, the web comic Coop de Grace, and book reviews. She is a graduate of Clarion–San Diego, class of 2007. When not writing, she throws pots, practices aikido, binds books, and plays with molten glass. She keeps a blog at www.catherinecheek.com.

Hands-on Handicraft:
The "DIY" Ideal

DIY: do it yourself. This handy little acronym has long been the Steampunk world's battle cry. It represents the attitude that draws many to Steampunk in the first place: a spirit of curiosity and independence, and a desire to slow down and make the world around us a little more intriguing.

"What better way is there to mix physics, history, and art (my three useless degrees)?" says Thomas Willeford. "People design fashion all the time. They draw a picture and say, 'It should look like this,' quite often not bothering to answer the question 'How does that stay on?' My interest in engineering makes it so that the first thing I wonder when I see something is physics: 'How is this going to work?' Art: 'How is it appealing?' And history: 'How is this Steampunk versus just assemblage art?' When I make something, I want people to look at it and almost believe it could have come from a specific year or time. I think one of the reasons

why I do well in Steampunk is that this background makes it so you can't just let yourself get away with things. The engineering has to look plausible (a piston on an arm has to look like it would actually manipulate that arm), the historic part has to look plausible (the Phillips screw is a twentieth-century design—I only use slotted screws on anything I intend to have been 'invented' in the Victorian era), and when I put a piece together, if the engineering works and it's historically appropriate (as opposed to accurate) but it's still butt-ugly, that would be a failure.

"I pretty much do it all myself. I have minions and lackeys to help me, and I encourage others to make their own stuff, but in the end it's all me. Now, being someone who makes all this stuff for a living, that may seem counterintuitive, but I feel that if someone buys something from me that they can't make themselves, that frees them up and gives them the time to do the things that they can."

Of course, for fans, tinkers, and cosplayers on a budget, sometimes DIY is the only affordable way to realize the creative vision. But even for many professional Steampunk artists, the DIY ethos informs their practice and is still totally essential to the creative work they do. "I do everything myself," says French artist and photographer Annliz Bonin. "I cannot stand not being in control of every aspect of my creation. . . . It is much more rewarding for me to create a work of art by myself, even if it isn't perfect. . . . I am interested in the path, not just in the outcome."

Libby Bulloff agrees. "[DIY] nearly always drives my work. I am a stubborn, underpaid autodidact, and therefore I am of a mind that DIY is the way to go. It's definitely more fun to teach myself, and often more affordable, though also at times less efficient than farming out the work to professionals or paying for formal education."

Working across varied mediums from drawing to installation, Louise Kiner is an accomplished artist—or, as she calls herself, an "art practitioner." This term expresses perfectly the practical attitude that characterizes Steampunk art and making: Being an artist isn't about who you are, it's about what you do. Among Kiner's most intriguing works are her "steam boxes," which house delicate arrangements of collage, sculpture, and found objects, frequently laid under glass. These collections of ephemera—pinned

OPPOSITE
Journal 1878 by Louise Kiner
ABOVE
The Airship "Mary Chickering" by Louise Kiner

insects, old maps, faded photos, scraps of antique cursive — evoke the atmosphere of another age. Kiner's work is quite hands-on, and she agrees that DIY plays a huge role in her work. "If I can't find the 'right' object, I have to find a way to make it from the bric-a-brac I have in my collections of found objects."

Kiner also discovered that sometimes a challenging project is just the thing to help a creator level up her skills from intermediate to master craftswoman. A friend of Kiner's offered her the use of a dilapidated dollhouse, discovered in the trash.

Because of the dollhouse's damaged condition, Kiner stripped it to a shell and rebuilt it: "I found myself consumed [with] researching how to restore different parts of it, as I had an idea in mind and the items I needed weren't readily available, so I had to make them."

Motivated by this big, challenging project, she has learned a lot along the way and picked up many new skills in the process. Now she can apply this broader knowledge base to her boxes.

"Right off the bat, problem solving and planning were the main things. Every time I pulled something away, I might find a crack that needed to be fixed or a structural problem that would need to be corrected. As far as planning goes, with a box, I was working on a smaller scale and a clean slate mostly; with restoring a doll's house, you are working on a bigger scale: six boxes housed within one bigger box. The exterior is as important as the interior. It's what makes people want to look inside. There is also a certain amount of having to manufacture things that weren't readily available; I wanted a slate roof. Real slate is available but costly. So I had to make it from scratch using painted egg cartons and a variety of cardboards. I want tapestries for some of the interior rooms, so I've had to learn how to do needlework to achieve this.

"I also had to learn how to use new tools, because most of the tools I had been using, such as X-Acto knives, were for working with paper. Now that I'm working with a variety of woods, I'm using a new variety of tools: hammers, saws, chisels, Dremels, a compound miter saw, et cetera. The skills are more woodworking skills."

Another artist with Steampunk ties who is particularly committed to developing her practice is Carrie Ann Baade. Her prolific body of work is primarily oil paintings and collage, and she is often associated with the pop surrealist movement.

Baade says, "My desire is to reclaim the past and preserve lost techniques for the future." Each composition can begin with hundreds of fragments from other works. "By cutting up images of old paintings and using them to create collages, I combined the power of these historical masterworks with my own experience as a contemporary artist. Using this fragmentary 'boneyard,' I took historical images that appeared meaningless and breathed new life — my life — into them." She adorns the collage in layer upon layer of paint, creating the illusion of three dimensions.

To complete her work, Baade draws on the oeuvre of past masters. But along with their material, she must also draw on their techniques, and that's

where the DIY comes in — Baade is learning artistic approaches that are no longer widely taught or conventionally appreciated. In a way, she is starting from the ground up, reinventing forgotten masterworks to stimulate the modern imagination, and excavating the past to create something totally new. "My reverence made me a scavenger salvaging lost aesthetics," she says, "but also a technician, who was researching processes and methods that were lost or underground during the twentieth century." Baade considers herself "a kind of Dr. Frankenstein attempting to piece together the sublime."

The result is works that are baroque and phantasmagorical and more than a little unsettling, dripping with reference to the mythical and the literary. But they also don't neglect the "punk" in Steampunk.

Punk also carries over into the process, in that, while DIY is rewarding, it can also get pretty messy. Unless you live with someone who likes a living room filled with paint, sawdust, and epoxy fumes, it can be difficult to pull off. If you're a dedicated DIY creator, you will need to make a serious effort to carve out room for artistic pursuits, in both your life and your living space. A workshop, garage, or studio? Even better!

ABOVE
Work in progress (detail) by Carrie Ann Baade.
OVERLEAF
Carrie Ann Baade's creative workspace.

OPPOSITE
Carrie Ann Baade, posing
with flamingo sculpture by
Jessica Joslin. Photo by
Lindsey Monteiro.
ABOVE
Jake von Slatt's Steampunk
Workshop.

Building a Steam-powered Orrery

by William Francis and Adrian Van Allen

The steam-powered orrery is composed of two tables—one table has the orrery itself with the planets and gearing, and the other has the steam engine and reduction gearbox. The second table isolates the engine vibration and the gearbox (625:1) reduces the ~700 rpm of the engine down to a bit over 1 rpm. The power is transmitted between the tables by a solid shaft into a bevel gear, which drives the gears on the top of the table. This example only goes as far as Saturn, which is common for orreries of the nineteenth century. The gear train was inspired by www.brassorrery.blogspot.com.

OPPOSITE
Orrery (work in progress) by William Francis and Adrian Van Allen.

1. CNC (computer numerically controlled) routing the gears and tabletop for the gearbox on a ShopBot. There is also a similar table bottom piece to make a sandwich the gears sit in.
2. An early test fit of some of the gearbox components.
3. The planets are driven by several concentric close-fitting tubes. Each is connected to one gear below. The bits of aluminum that hold the planet arms to the tubes are CNC cut.
4. Test fitting the planet gear train. Power from the steam engine drives the four gears on the far right. Those gears are solidly connected together, which in turn directly drives the first four planets in the solar system via the concentric planet tubes. Jupiter and Saturn require the extra gears to significantly step down their rotation from the first four.
5. The inside of the gearbox required a lot of custom hardware collars and spacers to get everything to fit correctly. Flanged bearings were used in

1.

3.

4.

5.

6.

7.

8.

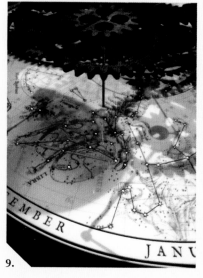

9.

10.

the uprights for very low friction. The uprights are held in place by small tabs of wood glued to the bottom. The top has similar tabs that hold everything secure when sandwiched together. The brass bosses that hold the wooden gears were machined on a lathe and soldered onto the shafts for a very solid connection.

6. Adrian designed a huge custom image made from lots of individual constellations. We set it to a large-format printer and very carefully glued the graphic to the orrery top. The graphic was intentionally designed to have the black border too large so we could cut to fit. The constellation stars had already been drilled out and filled with small amounts of the epoxy we would later cover the entire top in.

7. About to glue together the top and bottom pieces. Fit is critical, so we installed the shafts that the gears will turn on to help ensure good alignment. Adrian is pointing to the bearings that hold the shaft coming in from the steam engine table that has the bevel gear on the end, which delivers power upward to the gears. The large holes in the bottom of the table allow access to install the lights. They have covers, so it works well in a dark room.

8. Almost finished! The table legs are now complete. The steam engine is installed, and connection between the gearbox table and orrery can be seen. Both tabletops have the graphics and epoxy applied.

9. Constellation stars lit by the three fluorescent lights underneath!

10. Will manually turning the orrery, as on this evening we couldn't get steam into the room.

....

William Francis is a designer and maker and one of the masterminds behind Kinetic Steam Works, the innovative nonprofit organization and maker studio known by Steampunks for its experiments with steam-powered kinetic art. Francis is also a professional software designer and a photographer whose work has appeared in a variety of publications. Adrian Van Allen is an artist and designer who co-founded *ReadyMade* magazine and has created exhibits and websites for the Exploratorium, NASA, the Smithsonian, and the Cleveland Museum of Art. She is also a PhD candidate in anthropology at UC Berkeley who has held a National Science Foundation Fellowship and is currently a fellow at the Smithsonian. Francis and Van Allen collaborated to design and build the steam-powered orrery, which was exhibited at Maker Faire in 2013.

Developing Your Steam-era Skills

Another fun part of doing it yourself: If you love creating Steampunk art, what might be agony for someone else should be pure bliss for you. It can

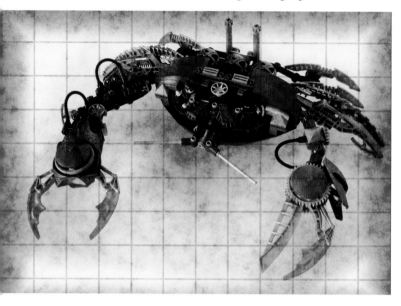

take a long, long time to develop the extensive body of skills needed to create polished, professional-looking work. Most retro-futurist artists and makers have invested a considerable length of time into learning their craft and honing their skills.

Libby Bulloff describes herself as a "self-taught creative," but she has also "received training along the way from other photographers, retouchers, designers, and editors," she says. "I've needed some rudimentary training in studio lighting, chemistry, and *patience* to get the tintype process to function. . . . Obsessive researching and fearlessly asking questions of people who know more than I do gets the process flowing."

Often, the Steampunk community helps provide the spark of inspiration. One of the people who assisted Bulloff along the way was Magpie Killjoy, founder of *Steampunk Magazine* and another well-known figure in the Steampunk scene. "When Magpie Killjoy came to town with his antique large-format camera, his trunk of dangerous chemicals, and his dreadlocked head full of knowledge and offered to teach me to make tintypes, I took to it obsessively. There is something about the stink of the ether and sandarac, the intensity of the light required, and the long exposures that just feels *right*. The process brings out this indescribable inner quiet in the models, and the resulting images are timeless and unpredictable. There are a million things that can go wrong, but when a perfect image appears, it's like a religious experience."

And Bulloff has continued learning. For instance, her recent discovery of wet-plate collodion photography, which she describes as "falling in love." Killjoy helped her out with some hands-on practice sessions, but Bulloff also took the opportunity to observe another local photographer, Dan Carrillo. Carillo is also an ambrotypist—the term for someone who works with wet-plate photography.

Mechtorian mastermind Doktor A also considers himself a lifelong learner, saying, "I pick projects that I am not entirely sure I can pull off in order to keep challenging myself and my abilities. I try and refine techniques and learn something new on each piece I make." Trained as an industrial

model maker, Doktor A worked for years as a designer and prototypist of toys, where he also picked up plenty of training on the job.

Like Doktor A, Louise Kiner accumulated a lot of her experience in the workplace, working as an FX assistant and animator. These days, when she wants to learn something new, she looks to the library or the Internet for research, or occasionally attends a workshop when she needs to study something specific. And, she says, "I have to admit that my husband, Pete, has been a great source when it comes to doing the more building sort of stuff. He's started to show me how to use some power tools so I don't lose any of my appendages."

While hands-on technical abilities (and dexterity with power tools) are important skills for every artist, for the retro-futurist artist it can also be important to learn both your science and your history.

"I think the more you understand an object and its function, the better you can depict it visually," says James Ng. "I studied the basic workings and the history of the steam engine and why it became so powerful. For other imagery that features machinery, a visual reference is almost always a must; I looked at modern and old tractors for my Harvester robot, propellers and zeppelins for my Imperial Airship, and the first steam-powered cars for my Bridal Carriage."

Some learn on the job, some pursue a formal arts education, while others are purely self-taught. But wherever they begin, the education never truly ends for most creators.

OPPOSITE
HMS *Shelman* by Guy Himber. "This crabby convey-ance can travel freely upon sandy shores and beached battlefronts."
ABOVE
Nautilus by Dr. Grymm
OVERLEAF
Flotilla by Ramona Szczerba

Making a Collaged Steampunk Stand-up Greeting

by Ramona Szczerba

While most of the artwork and illustration work I do is on canvas or water-color paper, or with objects, sometimes I like to invent an extra-special something for family, friends, and occasions. Recently I have been making stand-up greetings—fancy collage work that you can perch on a bookshelf or desk—just a little something beyond a greeting card. The Ambassador of Occasions, pictured here, is an example. She's not too hard to whip up, and you can opt to make her wings move, and dress her up after your own fashion with sparkles and bits you may have lying around. You can customize her banners to suit your occasion—and include her Steam Cake if it happens to be a birthday. So round up some supplies and let's get her started!

YOU'LL NEED

Images
Sharp scissors
White glue
Heavy black card stock or foam core
Pencil
Craft knife
Toothpicks
4 small brads
3-inch self-adhesive easel back (or make your own)

ADDITIONAL AND HELPFUL

Walnut ink or strong black tea
Colored pencils
Silver-ink gel pen
Tweezers
Small hole punch
Glue pen
Small gears, specialty brads, glitter, feather

INSTRUCTIONS

Carefully cut out all of the images. You can spritz the banners with walnut ink to age them if they look too white; you can also use strong black tea. Let them dry thoroughly, then add your messages. Glue the goggles to the hat and the hat to the lady. Maneuver the banner into her hands, and glue. You can add a little color to her with the colored pencils, if you like. Glue the lady toward the bottom of a piece of black card stock or foam core. With a pencil or the silver gel pen, create a base at the bottom for her to stand on, as shown. Make a small slit in the cake with the craft knife and insert the butter knife image. Add tabs to the bottom of the cake for the wheels, as shown. Add the banner to the balloon and glue down. Glue all the rest of the pieces to the card stock, placing the balloon off by itself a bit. Add tabs

1.

2.

3.

4.

5.

6.

7.

8.

9.

10.

to the wings, as shown. When dry, cut out the balloon. Trace around it with a pencil on some scrap card stock and cut that out, too. Glue the rest of the sheet of images to a second sheet of card stock, weigh it down with some books, and let dry thoroughly.

1, 2. Making the balloon: Run a bead of glue down the balloon's black shadow. Set a toothpick on the glue and press firmly. Put glue on the back of the balloon image and press it around the toothpick onto the black backing. Let dry.

3, 4, 5. Making the wings: Cut out the images from the black card stock. To attach the Ambassador's wings, make small holes in both of the wing tabs and in her shoulders with the craft knife, as shown. Slip a brad into the front of each of her shoulders and through the wing tabs. Fasten firmly in the back.

6, 7, 8, 9, 10. Making the cake: Poke through the center of the wheels and the tabs with a craft knife as with the wings. Thread a brad through a gear, then through the wheel, and attach to the cake, fastening in the back. Glue the propeller to the back of the plate, in case of flooding.

....

When **Ramona Szczerba** (aka Winona Cookie) is not being a psychologist in private practice in San Diego, she enjoys creating whimsical children's illustrations in watercolor, but also loves working with collage and assemblage. Her artwork and short stories have appeared in several publications, including *The Steampunk Bible*, and can be seen at www.winonacookie illustration.com.

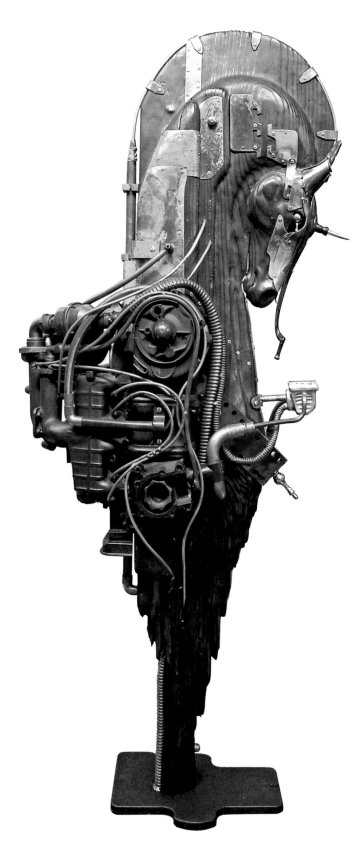

Meeting Challenges: The Methodical versus "Happy Accidents"

Every beginning creator is familiar with the seemingly insurmountable gap that arises between one's vision of the piece and its final execution. As Pierre Matter says, "There's always a fight between what's in your mind and what you're able to formalize through your hands and skills," a constraint that he definitely experiences as a sculptor. "In sculpture, you have to make the audience feel the essentials all at once. I go through with anguish and apprehension. The victory never lasts for long."

Whatever your medium, the goal of any arts practice is to develop a greater set of skills for dealing with challenges. Experience will help you close that gap between your own vision and the piece's final execution. So will extensive exposure to the work of a wide variety of other artists. In other words: Don't confine yourself to studying only the work of other retro-futurist artists and makers. Make a habit of visiting every museum of art and design possible, and viewing collections online. You may even find that problem-solving approaches from other creative forms will help you view your artwork in a whole new way (so keep turning pages!).

James Ng recommends looking for outside inspiration when you get stuck.

"If a person has a good idea but is having difficulties executing it, my advice would be to look at similar things that have been done before, and what made them work," he says. "What did other people do to bring their creation to life, to make it believable? It could be the context in which the creation is made, or how it is based on realistic scenarios or existing contraptions in our world."

Mimicry and modeling are in some ways the queen mother of Steampunk invention, after all—everything recycled and reworked and rethought from year to year. What once blossomed in prose in the 1980s may rise again in a painting or keyboard modification today, completely transformed by time and another creator's point of view.

Still, even for experienced artists, every creative project has its more specific challenges—the kind that require taking a wrench to the side of a robot or redoing schematics.

As with most things, the learning process requires a whole lot of patience, and even more hard work; it takes some elbow grease to get the creative gears turning smoothly.

Testing out a variety of approaches and seeing what works best, and documenting what you've done, will help fix not just the existing problem, but future ones as well. Doktor A says, "I come up against technical problems all the time. For example, how to get knee joints to work in a way that gives a piece an implied gait without impeding its support value. Or what material to use for a part to get the look I need with the strength or flexibility required. These are all just research and development issues. You prototype parts and try a few different methods to see what works best, and you learn things that you can use and build on in the future."

Danny Warner follows a similar method. "I'm schooled in typical design process; it's iterative. Stuff is made by testing and failing and learning in order to evolve the strongest possible solution at the end. So there's usually very little 'preciousness' in the middle of the design process."

Is it any wonder that some version of the scientific process works well in a pseudoscientific culture like Steampunk? That said, even Warner admits, "I don't try to force creativity, even if things just don't feel quite right."

Sometimes, it's best to just take a break. "If I find that I'm stuck on something, I usually will walk away from it and work on something else," says Louise Kiner. "If it's frustrating me, I'll head over to our local community center and swim a whole load of laps to clear my head. Strangely enough, I sometimes get my best ideas while swimming."

Kiner also discusses the value of the "happy accident," another scenario when it can be useful to take five, and return to the project with a fresh perspective. "Sometimes I'll do something unintentionally—like glue something in the wrong place, for example—and will have to correct it in some manner. At this point, I'll probably walk away from it for a while. Coming back to it some time later, I usually find I like it better, as now I've had a chance to look at it with a fresh eye."

No matter how bulletproof your process, there are going to be days when things just don't go according to plan. Carrie Ann Baade suggests that the antidote to discouragement is learning something new. "Recently, I learned to do handstands, and now it's hula-hooping. It's keeping a sense of play that prevents one from taking it all so seriously. Play is the fertile field where invention and wonder evolve . . . not the overplanted soul of achievement."

"Work, work, and work. It's sweat, and discipline. And if you fight against a blank slate, then it may be that it's too early, and you should accept that you are not ready yet," says esteemed Dieselpunk artist Sam Van Olffen. "But not being ready today doesn't mean you won't be ready later. You must be patient. *Ars longa, vita brevis*. 'Art is long, life is short,' as said exactly by Hippocrates."

The purest advice comes from Herr Döktor, however, who suggests a tried-and-true Victorian method for keeping a cool head: "I make a cup of tea or go for a walk."

Seven Pieces of Advice for New Artists and Makers

Are you a budding creator who is starting out with big ideas but a blank slate? Here are seven pithy pieces of wisdom to get you going. Some of it may be contradictory—and that's perfectly okay. Everyone's approach is different.

1. "START *small* and BUILD up to the big; don't be afraid of criticism, and keep on going. Practice is what it's all about." —*Herr Döktor*

2. "Get one of those really cheap, lined NOTEBOOKS (six by nine and a half inches is a good size) and *write* down or roughly *sketch* out any IDEAS you have. This is strictly a way of getting your ideas down quickly, without feeling any pressure to make gorgeous drawings, as it's not a 'sketchbook,' but an 'ideas book.' No one has to see it but you. . . . Work on the projects that you feel ready for, and add notes to your future projects on the skills you might want to learn or the supplies/ephemera you might need."

—*Louise Kiner*

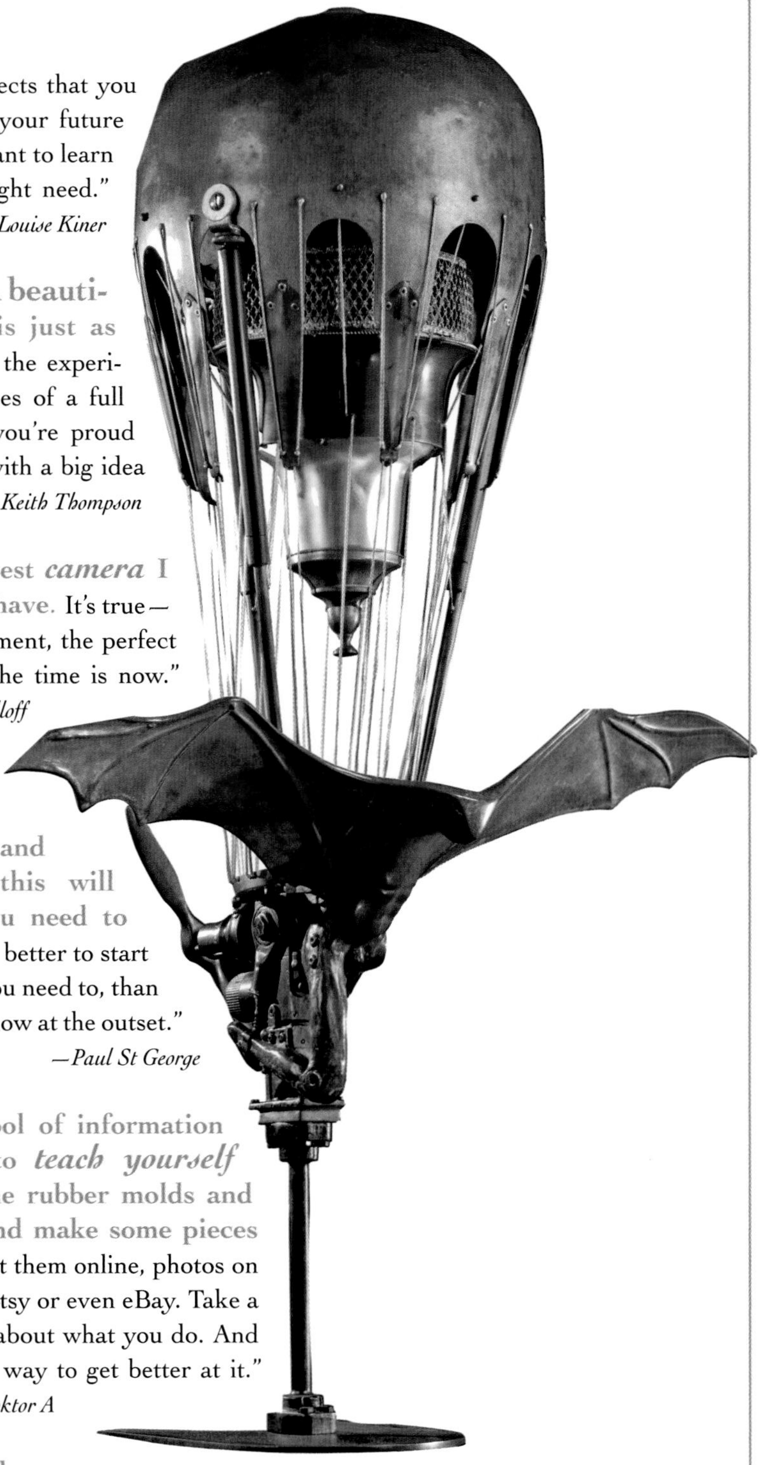

3. "Shelve the big ideas for now. A beautifully realized small idea is just as important. A big idea deserves the experience, craftsmanship, and resources of a full slate. With enough small ideas you're proud of, you'll suddenly find yourself with a big idea already underway."

—*Keith Thompson*

4. "Someone once told me the best *camera* I could get is the one I already have. It's true—you can't wait for the perfect moment, the perfect opportunity, the perfect setup. The time is now."

—*Libby Bulloff*

5. "*Keep* FAITHFUL to your big idea, and as you learn more about the context and audience for your work, this will provide the content that you need to further define your work. It is better to start big and then hone your work as you need to, than to reduce your idea to what you know at the outset."

—*Paul St George*

6. "Do it yourself. Use the pool of information ONLINE or in BOOKS to *teach yourself* how to weld or make silicone rubber molds and cast in resins or *whatever* and make some pieces yourself. Show them around. Put them online, photos on social media sites and maybe on Etsy or even eBay. Take a booth at a convention and shout about what you do. And keep doing it, a lot! It's the only way to get better at it."

—*Doktor A*

7. "NEVER *underestimate* the benefit of just spending **hours** and hours sitting at your workbench and **playing** around with materials and processes. It's all experimentation in the end, and as I said—there's rarely any instructions on how to build the things I and people like me create."

—*Mark Cordory*

Thomas Willeford's
Steam-powered Mecha-Penguin

by Scott Miller

To one-up the Sultan's Elephant from Jules Verne's classic novel, we set a challenge for Steampunk maker extraordinaire Thomas Willeford: Come up with a scale model for a functional steam-powered penguin—a *giant* steam-powered penguin. Herein you will find what was wrought, with the startling pics to prove it.

Along the way, we also turned to a few friends and colleagues who weighed in with their related expertise. Engineer Jon Marshall provided us with a helpful jumping-off point, commenting: "An thing large and steam-powered would have to ventilate a lot of heat, which, if it were standing on a glacier, would cause the ice to melt and the device to sink. So it would need to very aggressively vent heat upward and have lots of insulation on the bottom. And I'm guessing it would be amphibious? I guess I would look at a Civil War–era submarine as a start and add legs or wheels." Meanwhile, we interviewed maker Jake von Slatt, tech consultant Luis Rodrigues, and automation expert Minsoo Kang on the pros and cons of creating a giant steam-powered penguin in the first place.

As an expert on the history of mechanical follies, Kang says, "It's wholly appropriate that the first example of such a mechanical folly that came to my mind was Charles Babbage's attempts to complete the Difference and the Analytical Engines, since Babbage has emerged as a Steampunk icon after William Gibson and Bruce Sterling imagined him completing both devices.

"In the recent construction of the Difference Engine by Doron Swade, it was revealed that, while Babbage got the basic design of the device correct, it could not have been built in Victorian England since it required gears of such fine and intricate nature that they were beyond the technical capacity of the time. In other words, that quintessential Steampunk technology could only have been made in our own time. To me, that anachronism is the perfect illustration of the contradiction at the heart of the Steampunk genre, which tries to look backward (the nineteenth century) and into the future (impossible technology) at the same time."

How high on the scale of folly does a giant Steampunk penguin rank?

Kang rates the folly level "high, in terms of its lack of practicality and sheer absurdity, but all that is more than made up for by its surrealistic grandeur. I can imagine a Steampunk story in which Raymond Roussel, F. T. Marinetti, and Marcel Duchamp become engineers rather than writers and artists."

One important part of building a giant mecha-penguin is considering exactly what size will work best. For von Slatt, "the size depends a lot on the environment. For instance, a penguin built for modern highway use could not exceed thirteen feet, six inches. However, a penguin built for use on the open range, or in a past era, could be a lot taller; I think fifty inches is probably a good target for a conventionally powered penguin. That would leave room for a crew of two to four in the head, and an observation deck just below that could comfortably hold a dozen or so folks. Looking at the penguin's skeleton, it's actually more birdlike on the inside than it is on the outside. The rib cage only comes up to about the middle of the penguin and then there is a very long neck. I'd mimic this 'design' with a lightweight outer skin loosely coupled to an interior skeleton containing the motive power and actuators."

As for locomotion, steam would do the work, but von Slatt points out that "the power, if we are limiting ourselves to technologies achievable with a nineteenth-century manufacturing infrastructure, will likely come from burning something. Coal would be a good choice, or perhaps peat, for a quaint Scottish appeal. Wood might be ideal if this were to be a logging penguin."

Power is, in fact, the key issue, says von Slatt. "I think the main issue is going to be power. We'll need to force-feed these boilers coal and air, and they are going to need to run hot and very near their theoretical limits. Penguineering will be a dangerous business, with most penguineers ending their careers in boiler explosions and general falling-over accidents caused by overeager helmsmen and inattentive observers."

Von Slatt says he would go "with two independent steam generators: a traditional boiler to power the steam cylinders for fast, gross movement of limbs, and a lightweight high-pressure automotive-type steam generator: running a hydraulic pump for slower high-torque motion. The limbs would be a combination of actuator types so that the legs could quickly get under the falling penguin, since controlled falling is what 'walking' really is."

What's definitely clear, according to von Slatt, is that the Victorians possessed the technology to compensate for any tipping-over issues. "Oh, yes! What we would be talking about would be a relatively small set of gyroscopes to sense the penguin's attitude. The gyroscope cages would be attached to valves that would provide input to what would essentially be a hydraulic analogue computer—perhaps a HAC 9000? If you will allow me vacuum tubes—the triode was invented in 1906—I could improve on what would be a rat's nest of copper tubing, valves, and actuators. Hmm . . . Come to think of it, copper tubing may not be up to snuff for the pressures involved, so some testing with steel tubing of the age would be advised."

As for possible setbacks, Kang believes there might be problems with "dizziness caused by the wobbly movement of the machine. Nineteenth-century doctors came up with a new disorder called 'neurasthenia,' which is caused by the shocks the human body suffers in its experience of modern technology. A condition called 'autopenguinasthenia' would have to be invented to describe the psychological consequences of prolonged exposure to the penguin machine. For reasons already mentioned, I see this device being more popular in the early twentieth rather than the nineteenth century, at the height of the activities of the surrealists."

But with the engineering elements squared away, what materials would be used to construct the penguin? Von Slatt suggests a skeleton of steel. "Steel is one of the strongest and lightest materials available, even today. Aluminum is only slightly better, but available only in small quantities at the time. For the skin, I think we'd want sheet stock of some sort. Perhaps copper, like the Statue of Liberty, but I'd like to keep the weight as light as possible, so maybe early aircraft–style doped canvas over wood. However, if this is to be a battle penguin, we would definitely want a sandwich of hardened steel, canvas, and mild steel to absorb and deflect the energy of incoming projectiles."

Airships might even be deployed, because, as von Slatt says, "The cockpit management tasks of this beast are going to be staggering! There will likely be a captain in charge, a helmsman responsible for 'walking the bird,' a gyroscopeteur who balances the beast, and an engineer and fireman commanding a crew of stokers down in engineering tending the boilers. But it will be the navigator plotting the course who will benefit most from the observer up in the 'crow's nest,' as the airship will become known. Note: The airship will need to be tethered to the penguin by a cable containing conductors for a telegraph sounder, made from some of the small amount of aluminum available at the time."

Another issue is whether the penguin should be given some form of artificial intelligence, dangerous though this might be.

Artificial intelligence expert Rodrigues says that a "semblance of intelligence" could be created by building "a simple reactive agent using nineteenth-century technology. Reactive agents merely respond to external stimuli with preset behaviors; they have no memory and usually keep no internal state. So they are not actually intelligent, but are very effective at *appearing* intelligent. Deliberative agents are at the other end of the spectrum and are far more sophisticated and too complex to build mechanically."

The main difficulty with this sort of intelligence "would be providing the penguin with a sufficient wide array of sensors to get those stimuli. Most existing sensors are electronic, so we have to look for the few that are mechanical and chemical. For example, you can have sensors based on older instruments like magnetic compasses, astrolabes, and thermometers.

"If you're not averse to introducing electricity, you could fit the penguin with microphones and have it track sounds above a certain threshold or following basic patterns (think voice commands from a human operator). I imagine a mecha-penguin would be quite a noisy machine, though, but I'd be willing to suspend disbelief about that. I suppose you could build a purely mechanical microphone, since sound is just vibrating air, but I don't know how that could work."

However, Rodrigues has no idea "how you could build more interesting stuff, like optical sensors, without electronics, and the photoelectric effect wasn't even fully understood until Einstein. There are light detectors that are essentially thermometers, but they're not sensitive or responsive enough, and would probably not even work properly inside a steaming steam-powered machine."

Rodrigues suggests that any inventor should "fast-forward a couple of decades and pick up sonar technology to allow the penguin to 'see' sound, although it would take electronic computers to do something useful with most of that information."

As for Kang, he was disappointed we didn't ask him about the giant penguin's nemesis, the "giant Steampunk walrus."

OVERLEAF RIGHT
*The Great Steam Colossus,
Sphen 1* by Thomas Willeford

THIS PAGE IS THE ONLY REMAINING RECORD OF THE MÜDPHLAPPE POLAR EXPEDITION OF 1891.

The rest of the journal was most likely burned by the base crew for warmth before they died. They were found in the base by the 1911 expedition.

After the Lord Lawrence "Lumpy" Lairdahs expedition in 1883 and the Baron Virgil Butterknuckles expedition in 1888 both ended in disaster trying to reach the South Pole, Lord Albert "Pudgy" Müdphlappe envisioned an ingenious plan that is guaranteed to succeed where these others have failed.

In his famous 1891 lecture tour to promote the expedition, he explained the subtle brilliance of his plan. Those other poor souls, may they rest in peace, lacked the extensive scientific knowledge needed for such an endeavor as the conquest of the South Pole. You need the proper vehicle. Dogsleds and a mechanical elephant? Of course they failed! Neither dogs nor elephants are native to the region. My research has shown that the most prolific vertebrate of that area is the noble penguin.

With your generous financial support, I will complete the construction of the great Steam Colossus Sphen I. Just like its living counterpart, Sphen I is a thing of amphibious wonder. Sphen I will gracefully glide through the water to the very edge of the southern continent and, imbued by me with a penguin's natural grace, it will traverse the Antarctic landscape to the pole with ease. We had hoped to launch from Cape Town on the twelfth of March, but the minor setback of the main boiler exploding during tests has pushed the date back to July tenth of this year; that is, with your gracious help, of course. The audience was electrified by His Lordships presentation, and several members sought to actually sign up for the expedition.

A supply ship had been sent ahead of the expedition to establish a base at the landing point. Regrettably, there was a two-week delay because of difficulty mounting the eight-inch gun, which would be necessary to fend off giant polar bears and huge walruses. By the time the Sphen I landed, the supply ship had left, and only two half-frozen scientists were left manning the base camp. When they were informed about the reason for the delays, one flew into a rage, screaming at His Lordship. Something about the complete absence of polar bears and walruses in the region. The other one merely died.

A group of four crewmen were assigned to stay at the base while the Steam Colossus was prepared for its inland voyage. As the majestic Sphen I stood there awaiting the adjustment of the huge counterweight mechanism that will enable it to walk with a penguin's subtle stride, a remarkable thing happened: A sizable colony of live penguins began to gather near the base of the great machine. At this, Dame Edith Weesleshague, who had signed on as the expedition's surgeon and stylist, postulated that this was a sign of sentience in these remarkable creatures, as they must be doing this because they saw the mighty vessel as the coming of their own penguin deity. This caused another short delay as the expeditions spiritual leader, the Reverend Stolescrue, had to be restrained after he began attacking the poor things, claiming they were heathens and deserved no better.

Finally, the mighty vessel was on its way, and the four crewmen watched its lights disappear into the snowstorm that was building in force, a small band of penguins following in its wake.

As researched by Thomas Willeford

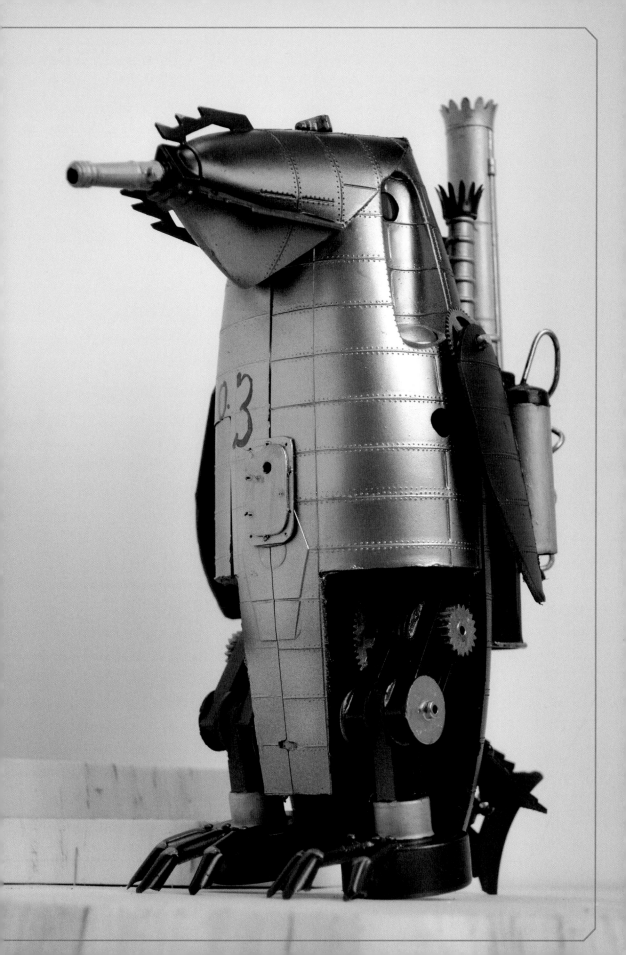

THE ENCYCLOPEDIA OF FANTASTIC VICTORIANA: ALTERNATIVE HISTORY EDITION.

DADD, RICHARD. Richard Dadd's fabulous painting "The Steam Dreadnought's Playground" shows an iron-clad steam mecha, poised in mid-step, perhaps to start racing forward toward the enemy's walls. The mecha is intently watched by a grotesque assortment of mechanical beings of all shapes and sizes. V.S. Naipaul, in *The Artist and the World: Essays*, says that the sense of the work is anticipation and terror. Time is suspended until the foot descends, and the foot is eternally about to descend. Dadd, says Naipaul, has painted "the moment when the breath is held, the moment that looks at an infinity of possibilities through utter stillness, so that time itself is not so much portrayed as annihilated."

In fact, Dadd's own life reveals an intricate combination of violence and annihilating stillness. In the early 1840s he was a successful young painter, known for his nature and fairy works, but during a tour of the Middle East a psychic episode completely changed Dadd's personality. He became increasingly violent and deluded, and on return to England he murdered his father with a knife. When he confessed to the crime he was sent away to the criminal department of Bethlem ("Bedlam") psychiatric hospital. There he painted several great works, including his masterpiece "The Fairy Feller's Master Stroke." In 1900 Dadd was approached by a young doctor, Thackeray T. Lambshead, who diagnosed Dadd with "VanderMeer's Chorea" and subjected him to an experimental treatment with Lambshead's "Steam Sane-itizer Helmet." Newly sane,

Dadd returned to the family estate and lived out the rest of his life.

It is hardly surprising that twentieth century critics have concentrated on the works produced during Dadd's incarceration, for the onset of VanderMeer's Chorea released Dadd's imaginative powers without impairing his technical skills. That Dadd's later return to sanity did not diminish either Dadd's output or his skills has never been disputed by these critics; but Dadd's new subject matter, the anthropomorphic and zoomorphic creations of the steam age, has never been in favor with the anti-imperialist and anti-military art critics.

The three works mentioned here date to after his years of mental crisis. The drawings are in watercolor and chiefly characterized by a fine technique, exemplified by the frequent use made of the point of the brush. The washes have been evenly applied and are carefully controlled, veering towards the more pallid tones of his later work. Flesh tones are under drawn with gray-green while the metal of the mechas has been treated with lighter shades of pink—almost flesh-colored. Light is hard and almost metallic in its luminosity. Details are meticulously rendered, while poses are stiff, outlines crisp, and shadows bold.

Painted in 1901, "The Steam Dreadnought's Playground" is a watercolor of a mecha in motion, brightly lit, around which steam crews and other mechas are crowded, all facing some figure or monument beyond the limits of the frame. Coal smoke obscures but does not entirely hide several of the mechas. The mecha crews stare out of the painting with mad, suspicious eyes, while the window plates of the mechas seem to have an unnerving, fixed mad stare. After the restoration of his sanity Dadd visited Pekin, following the suppression of the Chinese Revolt, and he was apparently taken by the sturdy iron figures of the mecha: "The mechanicals are very capital subjects for the brush; they rush along with great celerity, bear burdens of no small size, and carry weapons of great fearsomeness." The almost molecular accuracy of his paintings is reflected in the acute detail shown: the nicks on the cannon and Maxim barrels, the scars on both metal and flesh, the bizarre array of uniforms from crews of different nations, the war-torn landscape underneath and behind the mechas.

Notable are two other paintings: "Flight Out of India" (1902–1903) and "Contradiction: Kitchener and Botha" (1904–1906). Like "The Steam Dreadnought's Playground," both paintings are crowded with figures, and all three seem to bristle with occult meanings. "Flight Out of India" has a huge file of Russian soldiers and mecha at a mountain pass. To the left there is a crowded forest of lances and rifles held by infantry and cavalry, to the right tents and groups of Pashtun watching in a reserved manner. In the foreground is a group of pale-skinned people who seem to represent the flight into Egypt—a woman with a swaddled baby, a bearded Joseph. But Moses and Aaron are nowhere to be seen. They are replaced by sinister-looking children bearing rifles and pointing at the Russian soldiers. The *leitmotif* of the painting is repeated images of points, on lance-heads, on mecha, on soldiers' helmets. In the very middle is a group of uniformed Russian officers, helmeted and red-vested. The central officer, the apparent commander, is drinking from a flask that obscures his face. The allegory of this ominous painting is a mystery. It is not the Israelites leaving Egypt, but something whose meaning is more obscure.

"Contradiction" is easier to read. Kitchener wears his full dress uniform. Botha is unexpected—an Arcimboldo agglomeration of tinier Boer figures, mecha, and symbols, wielding a rifle and crushing to death one of a group of tiny Zulus who are dashing around his feet. Botha's face is sullen; he stares up and away from Kitchener. The entire painting is crammed and crowded with a typically Daddian mixture of intricately-detailed figures and mecha on all scales—a tiny battle between English mecha and Boer snipers, a Zulu *assegai* in mid-flight next to Botha's head. A mysterious mecha of unrealistic design scales a far-off mountainside; on top of the strange mecha is a tiny hanging green fairy. As in "The Fairy Feller" and "Steam Dreadnought's Playground" there are variegated plants, grasses, weeds, randomly over the surface of the work, and delicately depicted mechas, about as tall as the miniature Zulus at Botha's feet. Everywhere you look, a face or mecha windshield looks at you, and the red of Kitchener's uniform and the bloated, drowned-man skin of Botha's face stand out strongly.

JESS NEVINS

STEAMPUNK DESIGN: FASHION, ARCHITECTURE, AND INTERIORS

Fashion, architecture, and interior design all speak to the ways in which we design our environments and ourselves. Fashion allows us to communicate our personalities and values through our appearance and our clothing; meanwhile, architecture and interior design let us communicate our personalities and values through our homes and workplaces, both inside and out.

Today, Steampunk and retro-futurism are providing both DIY and professional designers with an expanded toolbox and a more sophisticated palette for expressing individuality and personal flair. "Steampunk has reintroduced an appreciation of beauty, craftsmanship, and detail into all areas of design, including industrial and interior decoration, by fusing fantasy with utility," says Jema Hewitt, one of the Steampunk scene's favorite costume and jewelry designers. (Hewitt has also written several books on Steampunk culture and design, with more hands-on projects and tips for the creatively inclined.) "Modern design has a tendency toward reductionism, paring away until just the functional minimum, the bleached bones, are left. Steampunk has put the muscle, skin, clothing, and trinkets back; the detail, the whimsy, the fun."

Many people have embraced the Steampunk aesthetic in their homes and in their personal attire simply because they love the way it looks. It's no surprise; the aesthetic is pleasing. For interiors, Steampunk design creates a welcoming atmosphere—accomplished craftsmanship, a cozy color palette, intriguing knickknacks, and well-aged antiques—offering styling that's simultaneously both rugged and opulent. For clothing, Steampunk represents a flexible and highly customizable range of looks and accessories, running the gamut from elaborate black tie and ball gowns to more serviceable, off-the-rack street wear.

For others, however, Steampunk design is a political statement. It's a fashion-forward way of turning something old into something new, saving both money and the environment in the process. Retro-futurism is a kind of cohesive set of design principles based around the edict "reduce/reuse/recycle." And it's a way of declaring that even if your shopping is limited to thrift stores, consignment shops, and other people's basements, you can still have a personal style of which to be proud.

PAGE 84
Styled by Jessica Rowell. Modeled by Ulorin Vex. Photo by Tas Limur.
OPPOSITE
Digital Grotesque (Grotto Side 1—Test Assembly) by Michael Hansmeyer and Benjamin Dillenburger. This structure is designed according to a complex mathematical algorithm and 3-D printed out of sand.
ABOVE
Dark Garden Corsetry. Photo by Joel Aron.

How Retro-futurism Is Influencing Fashion, Architecture, and Interior Design

Fashion

From head-to-toe costuming (complete with props), to cutting-edge couture, to more practical everyday wear, Steampunk style is incredibly versatile. The look is making waves at convention costume contests and on the catwalk, and it's also influencing broader style trends. Nowadays, well-dressed hipsters are sporting suspenders, leather boots, vintage dresses, handlebar mustaches, and elegant updos. In other words, retro-futurism offers a sartorial gold mine of exciting new looks.

For costume designer Paige Gardner Smith, necessity was the mother of invention, as she also longed to both create and live her retro-futuristic vision. She dreamed of creating Victorian-style working automatons, but did not possess the skills or the resources to set up a full-scale fabrication and welding workshop. So instead, she turned to the use of costuming and props to replicate the look and feel of an automaton as best she could, and began creating and performing the automaton character herself, using her own body as the canvas. "Using simple hacks to repurpose salvaged items into elements of costuming, I am able to immerse myself—figuratively and literally—in Steampunk design. The ability to express myself artistically, using my own form as a frame, continues to inspire every new project. The fact that I can 'inhabit' what I build remains the most compelling aspect of every costume journey."

Other approaches include designer Amanda Scrivener's philosophy of starting with the accessorizing: "Combining vintage or historical styles

OPPOSITE
Dark Garden Corsetry. Photo by Joel Aron.
ABOVE
Wooden Bunny with Brass Wings by Amanda Scrivener

and punking those up!" Scrivener's diverse talents in textiles, metal, and leather shine through in her one-of-a-kind creations, which definitely bring together the daintily vintage and the rebelliously punk into one boldly embellished package. Scrivener markets her bespoke accessories via her steamsona, Pro-fessor Maelstromme. Looking to the future, she says: "We have already seen design-ers on the catwalk incorporating traditional countryside dress, tweeds, and plaids with strong adventure influences. I can see it will go mainstream, too, as you can take from it smaller elements of the style."

Of course, while some designers might interpret the Steampunk aesthetic with an emphasis on "countryside chic"—something like what a gathering of fashion-forward Vic-torian ladies and gentlemen might wear on a hunting party in the woods—there are plenty of other ways to play it. Though the landed gentry and the convention-bucking adventur-ers dominate our tales of the Victorian era, the fact is, the vast majority of people then were working-class or middle-class, just like now. There were servants and waitstaff, stable boys and scullery maids, coal shovelers and factory workers, not to mention lawyers, doctors, and ministers and their daughters and wives. It was a particularly regi-mented time, and each of these individuals had their own established style of dress. Sure, it's probably more fun to dress up as a wealthy lady than a scullery maid. But high fashion does not demand any particular allegiance to the historicity of a particular costume; there's no reason a developing Steampunk fashion sense can't draw on details and inspiration from the nineteenth century's total range of social experience.

Part of the process of becoming accomplished as a designer is develop-ing your own distinctive vision, a personal vernacular in which to fluently express your aesthetic sensibilities. And, as Jema Hewitt points out, these sensibilities don't just vary from person to person; there is also a geographic element. Steampunk fashion also varies from place to place, with different cultures interpreting their visions of the past in unique ways.

Hewitt says, "I've really noticed a huge difference around the world in the way different groups dress, so in the UK there is an emphasis on beautifully made Victorian gowns with carefully researched patterns and natural fabrics; there's also a lot of genuine Victorian military uniforms. In Scandinavian Steampunk, there is more leather, metal, and studs—almost an armored look—while lots of American neo-Victorian costume seems to be more angled toward fantasy with a sense of playfulness, often using very modern materials and color palettes, recognizable characters or themes."

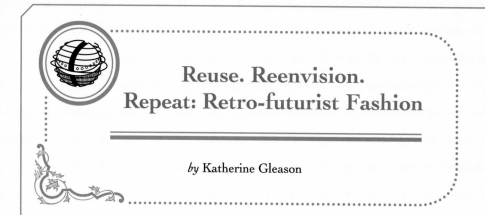

Reuse. Reenvision.
Repeat: Retro-futurist Fashion

by Katherine Gleason

Fashion designers have long mined the past, studying historic looks and adapting them to the present. Sometimes these forays result in technologically advanced outfits that look as if they come from out of an idealized past. A few luxury brands have produced notably retro-futurist lines. Nicolas Ghesquière, head designer at Balenciaga from 1997 to 2012, was lauded for imparting a modern sheen to his house's futuristic design archive. Many Steampunks pointed with knowing pride to Prada's Fall 2012 menswear campaign, which featured actors Willem Dafoe, Gary Oldman, Garrett Hedlund, and Jamie Bell attired in ensembles that would delight a retro-futurist gentleman. Alexander McQueen's fashions have often drawn upon a Victorian or Edwardian silhouette, incorporating bustles, padded hiplines, corsets, and tiny cinched-in waists. These shapes, coupled with the original designer's interest in science, technology, and innovative textiles, resulted in a particular and distinctive brand of retro-futurist creation.

Lee Alexander McQueen, founder of the Alexander McQueen label, was a hero to so many. Before his suicide in 2010, fashion students and aspiring young designers either wanted to work for him or to be him. Known for his sharp tailoring and theatrical runway shows, McQueen was hailed as a genius, and at the same time, he was often referred to as the "bad boy of British fashion."

Born into a working-class London family—his father drove a cab and his mother was a homemaker—the young McQueen evinced an early interest in fashion. At the age of three, he drew Cinderella in a voluminous ball gown on the wall of his sister's room. Despite his desire to study art, McQueen left school as a teen and worked as an apprentice at Anderson & Sheppard, a leading Savile Row tailor. After a few years, he moved to Gieves & Hawkes, another respected Savile Row establishment. At Bermans & Nathans, the renowned costumers, McQueen learned to cut historic patterns, working on the clothing for the London stage production of *Les Misérables*. Changing gears again, McQueen landed a job with avant-garde designer Koji Tatsuno, whose label was backed by the internationally lauded Yohji Yamamoto. Tatsuno, who had a small boutique in Mayfair, describes his studio of the late 1980s as a hangout spot for young designers, including McQueen and Julien Macdonald. "I gave them space to be freely

OPPOSITE
Jill Anderson's Viking Jacket, crafted from gold leaf brocade with snap details, blends history with technology. Modeled by Erina Davidson. Photo by Meredith Zinner Photography.

creative," says Tatsuno. "Many of them didn't go to school, and I'm very happy that many of them later on became great designers." McQueen also worked for John McKitterick, designer of the label Red or Dead and the creator of the anatomically correct gay Billy doll, and was a design assistant for Romeo Gigli in Milan.

With all this on-the-job training under his belt, McQueen applied for a position teaching pattern cutting at Central Saint Martins College of Art and Design. Bobby Hillson, the head of the college's MA fashion course, liked McQueen's portfolio. Instead of offering him a job, though, she offered him a place as a student. McQueen enrolled in the course and, sixteen months later, presented his graduate collection with the class of 1992. McQueen's six-outfit collection, which was inspired by Jack the Ripper's female victims, incorporated fashion elements from the 1880s along with avant-garde flourishes. Isabella Blow, the noted stylist, was fascinated by McQueen's work and famously purchased the whole collection on an installment plan. Blow became McQueen's promoter and muse, wearing his clothes on the streets of London and in the pages of *Vogue*.

"Nihilism," Alexander McQueen's Spring 1994 collection, received the designer's first professional catwalk show. His scantily clad models, who appeared to be smeared with blood, shocked the audience and got the attention of the press. McQueen's next collection, "Banshee" (Fall 1994), further explored retro-futuristic themes—a pregnant skinhead with McQueen's name inked in silver on her shaved head modeled a sheer black dress with a revealing Elizabethan neckline, while another model sported a perfectly tailored Victorian-style frock coat with metallic lapels over bare legs and a pair of transparent plastic boots. The crowd and the press enthused about McQueen's work, the *Observer* dubbing him the "star of the week."

Over the years, McQueen's shows grew into increasingly elaborate and controversial affairs, resembling performance art and the fine art of the period. Despite any controversy, the fashion establishment had its eye on McQueen. In October 1996, McQueen was appointed head designer at Givenchy. McQueen took up the reins at that venerable Parisian house and continued to design his own line, producing six collections a year. Shortly after his appointment at Givenchy, McQueen won the British Designer of the Year award from the British Fashion Council. He was recognized by the BFC three more times—in 1997, 2001, and 2003. In October 2003, he received a Commander of the Order of the British Empire medal from Queen Elizabeth II.

After leaving Givenchy in 2001, McQueen expanded his company and continued to produce innovative and often disturbing runway shows for his own label. While his shows often incorporated gothic elements—skulls, bones, and other macabre details—his designs also embodied a retro-futurist aesthetic. The punk princesses who paraded around a silk-wrapped tree during the first half of his Fall 2008 ready-to-wear show displayed crinoline frocks and precisely cut military tailcoats along with a bold, forward-looking attitude. For both Spring 2009 and Spring 2010, McQueen created digitally engineered prints inspired by evolution, which were sewn into his signature shapes—corset dresses, frock coats, and narrow-legged pants. In addition to being retro and futuristic, the Spring 2010 collection also had a dystopian theme. McQueen imagined a time when the polar ice caps have melted, and humans, with the aid of bioengineering, have returned to the sea.

Numerous independent and regional designers also create in a retro-futurist vein: Samantha R. Crossland, who has worked under the Blasphemina's Closet label and is now producing under the name Samantha Rei; Zoh Rothberg, whose Morrigan New York, a Brooklyn-based design studio, puts out gothic Lolita looks and will soon be producing Victorian-style garments, incorporating high-tech fabrics; and Philadelphia-based Autumnlin, who designs both Heartless Revival, a ready-to-wear line, and Autumnlin Atelier, limited-edition garments. Jill Anderson debuted her eponymous label in Athens, Greece, in 1989. Six years later, she opened a boutique in Manhattan's East Village, which came to be known as the go-to shop for artistic and intellectual women.

Anderson focuses on wearability and functionality, drawing inspiration from working women of the past, historic garments, and vintage fabrics. Her Italian Widow Dress, a shop best seller, has become a retro-futurist uniform for many. The dress, which was inspired by Anderson's experience of living abroad, features a narrow sleeve, which allows for ease of movement. The designer explains that a more fitted sleeve and shoulder line, which are typically found in vintage garments, facilitate movement of the arm, a necessary function for working women of all eras. Inspired by E. J. Bellocq's photographs of New Orleans prostitutes in the early twentieth century, Anderson created her Parachute Dress, which has become a staple of downtown weddings and can also be dressed down and worn to the office. The Parachute Dress, with its fitted bodice and full-flounced hem, echoes a Victorian silhouette and thus has caught the eye of many a Steampunk lass. All of Anderson's handmade creations feature her signature architectural construction paired with vintage allusions, resulting in timeless styles that capture the best of yesterday and tomorrow. Sadly, escalating rents forced Anderson's brick-and-mortar store to close in November 2013. But her designs live on, on the streets of New York and possibly soon in the digital realms of cyberspace.

ABOVE
Jill Anderson's Italian Widow Dress in autumn-hued plaid flannel. Modeled by Raven Jensen. Photo by Meredith Zinner Photography.

....

Katherine Gleason is the author of *Anatomy of Steampunk: The Fashion of Victorian Futurism* and *Alexander McQueen: Evolution*, a book about the late designer's runway shows.

Architecture and Interior Design

It's taken on a number of different forms, but minimalism in one expression or another has been the dominant aesthetic in architecture and interior design for some time. Now Steampunk offers a vivid counterpoint and welcome contrast, along with its associated subgenres like Dieselpunk, Rococopunk, Noirpunk, and so on. These rich and visually stimulating looks draw on the baroque sensibilities of the Victorians and the heavily ornamented styles of art nouveau, or the gritty aesthetic of up-and-coming industry: burnished concrete, cracked brick, and exposed pipes.

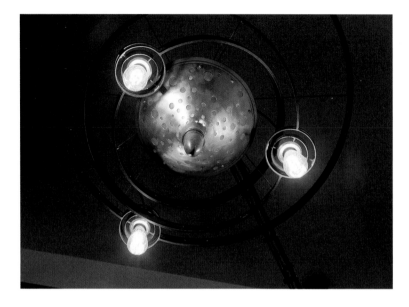

Taken by itself, the "industrial look" has been around for quite a while. As designer J. W. Kinsey puts it, "It has not arrived, as it has never left: It has been here since Victorian England and the Industrial Revolution." It's an aesthetic born of total practicality; the brick buildings of yesteryear were built to last, to withstand winter and summer, fire and flood. And in many old city centers, they have lasted indeed, standing firm and proud while more recent construction has fallen into decay. Now these old industrial buildings are being refurbished, renovated, and reclaimed to beautiful effect, another one of retro-futurism's sneaky influences on the outside world.

Art Donovan is best known for his inventive and elegant lighting designs. "Steampunk was the perfect storm of all my previous experiences," he says. "When I was four, I was so obsessed with the imagery of the old gaslit Sherlock Holmes movies that I made a makeshift deerstalker hat out of my brother's baseball caps—complete with an oversized magnifying glass (a paper plate)." After this early foray into Steampunk craftsmanship, Donovan became an avid fan of science fiction films, and went on to become a designer and illustrator for sci-fi-centric toy companies. Later, his designs began to incorporate an art deco aesthetic. He concludes: "There was always a vintage or historic influence in my work, but Steampunk was that unique spark that tied together *all* of my lifelong enthusiasms."

When it comes to retro-futuristic interiors, Donovan's expertise is impressively extensive. He describes the industrial aesthetic as "the simpler, real-world version of Steampunk." According to Donovan, this look has been in vogue for nearly forty years. "In the late 1960s, niche retailers like United House Wrecking were offering all manner of vintage industrial,

farm, and nautical detritus for accent pieces and furnishings. In the seventies and eighties, old industrial urban lofts were being converted for full-time art studios and residential use—complete with exposed plumbing pipes, overhead doors, and exposed structural beams and electrical conduits. It's evident that this raw, industrial aesthetic has been firmly established in interior design. But the new Steampunk design movement goes well beyond this original visual vocabulary. It's much more technically based and heavily infused with nineteenth-century science fact and fantasy elements." In other words, the special sauce that takes a space from merely industrial to genuinely retro-futuristic often lies solely in the judicious use of accessories.

Tanya Clarke is another lighting designer whose "Liquid Light" assemblages create the impression of a drop of water, brightly illuminated from within and poised infinitely on the edge of falling—a look as fanciful and surreal as it is industrial. Clarke comments, "Just as the world is becoming more and more blended, an attraction toward a blending of aesthetics is occurring. Steampunk seems to embrace this attraction by blending textures and natural materials in a 3-D format, with the added flair of theatricality."

In fact, theatricality is a great lens through which to view the Steam-

punk look. It's that melodrama, that enigmatic sense of both narrative and performance, which sets Steampunk apart from other design approaches. At times, the impression can be almost intimidatingly immersive, especially in cases where enterprising designers have created interior spaces outfitted in Steampunk style from baseboards to rafters and wall to wall (more on this shortly). The effect is enchanting and magical, but it can also be a bit overwhelming. A "fully loaded" Steampunk space tends to oversaturate the senses; its brassy look is better for a high-gloss photo spread than a much lived-in living room.

Most, however, are using retro-futurism as just one element in their interior design. As Art Donovan explains, "Some enthusiasts would surely love to live the fantasy 24-7, but that is akin to living in a theme park (and that's not the desire of my own architectural clients). My personal rule of thumb for how much of a rich, aggressive style to employ in any given environment is directly proportional to the amount of time someone spends in that environment." Donovan offers the example of a restaurant, where each patron may only spend a couple of hours at a time, and the Steampunk elements can be a lot more aggressive: "You have much more flexibility in adding richer and more eye-popping details." Likewise for a hotel lobby or other public-use areas. "But since homes and apartments are where we spend the greatest part of our life, Steampunk is *most* effective when used sparingly and in combination with an eclectic mix of details and complementary finishes. Here the last thing I'd want to see is overkill in a Steampunk design application. . . . Keeping all these considerations in mind, I believe Steampunk is now clearly a strong and desirable style for artwork and interior design elements."

Bruce Rosenbaum espouses a similar principle. Rosenbaum is the founder of ModVic, a Steampunk art and design company. ModVic—short for Modern Victorian—grew out of an epic restoration project that he and his wife, Melanie, undertook on their own Victorian Craftsman-style home, originally built in 1901. Together, they founded ModVic in 2007, and it has grown into a successful design and consulting firm. Their design theory is based on the idea of combining opposites—like blending today's cutting-edge technology with the atmospheric elegance of Victorian design.

Rosenbaum says, "My creative design process employs 'Janusian Thinking'—the combining and synthesizing of opposite ideas (think of a hammer—pounding and removing nails in one single object). Steampunk design is the essence of Janusian Thinking and creates a creative problem-solving process that is wide open—with no self-imposed barriers or restrictions." Both in life and in design, balance is indispensable, particularly when taking retro-futuristic design to the mainstream.

On the other hand, there are times when it's just better to go a little overboard. On the next few pages, we profile two striking spaces where the designers followed their instincts and pushed Steampunk to its limits.

Three Rings Interior —
Because We Can

ABOVE
Office space by architectural
and design firm Because We
Can for game development
studio Three Rings in San
Francisco.
OPPOSITE ABOVE
Three Rings staff members
store their bikes in a space
designed to resemble an
engine room.
OPPOSITE BELOW
The Three Rings game room
is designed for on-site rest
and relaxation.

Because We Can is an architecture and design studio in Oakland, California. Originally led by husband-and-wife team Jeffrey McGrew and Jillian Northrup, the studio has now grown into "a five-person powerhouse." They describe the shop as "a new kind of architecture firm: a Design-Build Studio." In other words, they both envision and execute the design, managing everything from brainstorming to production. To do this, they draw on the varied skills of architects, builders, fabricators, and even a few robots in their high-tech fabrication shop.

Northrup says, "We pride ourselves in being able to produce just about anything. We do not limit ourselves to the initial ideas of what can and cannot be done. We think first about what would make the project the absolute best it can be. Then we figure out how to make that happen. We use the latest technology in software and digital fabrication to add efficiency and ingenuity to every project."

Perhaps because of their DIY attitude, the shop has been especially popular with clients aiming for a retro-futuristic aesthetic, with projects such as the "Mad Scientist Home Workshop," a fantastical workspace built into a private residence, or the "Long Now Salon," a remodeled event space for the Long Now Foundation that suggests the best intellectual gathering places of yesteryear.

One of our favorite projects, however—and one of the shop's first undertakings—is the office of Three Rings, a game development studio in San Francisco. Northrup says, "The main reason for this office was to create an amazing and fun space for the staff to work in that would inspire and delight." The idea they finally hit on was fully Steampunk, with a heavy dose of inspiration taken from the interior of Jules Verne's *Nautilus.*

Once again applying the principle of DIY, Three Rings' employees had a chance to design and customize their own desks using a template provided by Because We Can. The shop also built a special gaming table, designed a bar for the lounge with Willy Wonka–esque levels of whimsy, and used ten-dollar off-the-shelf lights from Ikea inside specially fabricated clawlike frames for lighting that

was both unique and affordable. There is even a special seating arrangement comprised of giant beanbags (the largest measures twenty feet long) that look an awful lot like squid tentacles; the throw pillows are adorable baby octopi. Surely, however, the space's coup de grâce is a bookshelf that swings aside to reveal a secret room hidden behind it—truly the makings of a Victorian genius's secret lair.

Northrup says, "We, of course, think architecture and interiors are very important and can be amazing, magical places. When we are designing, we are just creating a place we want to be, or a place we feel the client wants to be. They are each their own magical pockets with their own surrounding feelings as you experience the space."

Truth Coffee Shop Interior — Haldane Martin

One of the most striking retro-futuristic interiors we've ever seen is Truth, a Steampunk-style coffee shop, bar, and restaurant in Cape Town, South Africa. While the Three Rings interior is fun, playful, and a little bit tongue-in-cheek, Truth's design, by innovative architect and designer Haldane Martin, is gritty, gorgeous, and as contemporary as it is vintage.

To begin with, Martin's firm chose a great canvas; the coffee shop is housed in a three-story warehouse building that dates back to the turn of the century. They stripped the building back to the essentials, exposing original stone, brick, and cast iron. The ground floor of this building houses Truth. "The old building that the Truth Coffee partners bought for their coffee roastery is in an edgy fringe district of Cape Town that is slowly transforming into a creative and innovative neighborhood," says Martin. "This area also happens to be the oldest part of Cape Town, dating back three hundred fifty years, and was the original shipping warehouse district before the new harbor was built. Truth Coffee HQ has become the new kingpin in this district by embracing the gritty, authentic past at the same time as bringing something unexpected and new. The fact that this is a working space—Truth Coffee roasts and distributes their coffee from here—keeps things real. The venue also works as an event space in the evenings, with the electro-swing scene taking full advantage of the Steampunk and low-light ambience. The space really enhances the fantasy, escapist purpose of a good party."

Truth's decor includes antique telephones, typewriters, and Singer sewing machines, collected by coffee shop owner David Donde. Donde is apparently somewhat of an inventor himself; he's currently working on developing a small-scale steam-powered cell phone charger. "One thing that retro-futurism highlights is all this old technology that is still around," says Martin. "As it has been around for a while, it tends to be quite economical. Repurposing it for new contexts and needs could create a lot of true innovation."

As a matter of fact, it was Haldane Martin's interior design intern Ruben Basson who came up with the idea of using Steampunk. "He put forward Steampunk as a conceptual reference when we were busy with the Truth Coffee concept stage," Martin tells us. "We showed it to our client, David Donde, and he loved it. He really identified with Steampunk, as he already was a crazy genius-inventor type. Now he had found a name for it."

The decor of the space revolves around the vintage roaster, a three-ton piece of machinery that is both totally beautiful and fully functional (a great principle for retro-futurism). Another major feature of the space is a twenty-five-foot communal table, built from industrial pipe and topped with Oregon pine reclaimed from the building itself. And the entire space is outfitted with purpose-designed seating, from overstuffed leather chairs to vintage bar stools.

"We were both clear that there would be no fake Steampunk decor applied to the space," says Martin. "This suited my more pared-down, modernist, Bauhaus-aesthetic inclinations, and this honest philosophy is also central to the Truth Coffee brand." However, he says, they always worked with fun in mind. "Even though we invested thousands of hours into this iconic Steampunk space, we don't take it too seriously. It's ultimately just another frivolous style that we all had fun exploring. Kind of like a fancy dress party."

The Future of Steampunk Fashion and Design: In with the Old *and* the New

Goggles and gears, pocket watches and brass keys are Steampunk's "clichés," but also an "easy shorthand," as Paige Gardner Smith puts it; they are translatable across all media and serve a purpose "much as peace symbols and neon flowers become quick iconic tags for hippie counterculture." Still, the ubiquity of these symbols can pose a dilemma for designers. How do you build on the familiar while moving past the mundane? Here are a few ideas.

Fashion

"One trend I'm happy to see evolving in alternate-history costume design is the use of bright colors," Smith says. "The 'go-to' palette of brown and brass is falling away. Costumers are really starting to taste the rainbow of color and hue, which permeated an era that was only *photographed* in sepia tones."

You'll find examples of nontraditional Steampunk color choices throughout this book, but thinking about color is just a start. Another way

to think about getting somewhere new is to let unusual items inspire you.

As artist and fashion designer Kristin Costa says, "I think people who wish to separate themselves as liking Steampunk as more than just a passing trend are starting to find fresh things to feature in their outfits and projects by digging more deeply through antique shops and searching a bit harder for their details. I personally love using antique hardware in unusual ways, and like seeing how other people do it as well."

Costa received her formal training at New York's Pratt Institute. Her interests are varied and her talents are versatile, extending from freelance costuming to a seasonal fashion line; her portfolio includes productions from television to puppetry. Her work is unified by a weirdly enchanting aesthetic that draws on retro-futurism in all kinds of interesting ways.

Costa has found opportunities to push boundaries with her holiday collection. "I am going . . . back to some pseudo-Victorian designs, inspired by Dickensian imagery of street urchins."

The aesthetic draws on the DIY and reduce/reuse/recycle aspects of Steampunk, and, according to Costa, is inspired in part "by the resourcefulness one needs when they are down on their luck." She adds, "This collection is inspired by all the times that I had to use supplies from my

grandparents' garage to create showpieces for projects because I couldn't afford supplies. There were times during art school where half the class's paintings were on the backs of cereal boxes or boards found in the dumpster because we couldn't afford good canvas. It has made me into a more resilient designer. I actively try to recycle now, but there were and probably always will be times in which it is necessary to elevate common materials into fashion because of financial restraints."

Smith is also experimenting with the use of reclaimed materials. Giving new life to old stuff is practical from a budgeting perspective, it's pragmatic considering our current environmental crises, and it can also make a powerful statement. Take, for example, Smith's *Tornado Jane* piece. This work incorporates debris that Smith collected in the wake of the tornadoes that devastated her home state of Alabama in April 2011.

OPPOSITE ABOVE
Eric Scotolati portraying
Feste in Curio Theatre's
Steampunk production of
Twelfth Night. Photo by Kyle
Cassidy.

OPPOSITE BELOW
Tornado Jane by Paige
Gardner Smith. Photo by Dim
Horizon Studio.

LEFT
Steampunk DevaDasis (2013)
by Suna Dasi, featuring Suna
Dasi and Meghan Ghent
(right). Photo by Art Attack
Films.

"It was almost therapeutic, looking past the devastation, wanting to see with new eyes, bits of wreckage that could reemerge as art," Smith says. "It was my hope to combine beautiful repurposing with haunting remembrance and give a second life to these disparate elements in the wake of that shocking disaster." *Tornado Jane* is a stately and somewhat inscrutable piece, following the "Victorian automaton" aesthetic that informs much of Smith's work. It reads as the regalia of a survivor, and its history gives it weight.

Smith adds, "Steampunk *is* recycling, in my estimation. We've taken a 'used' era, refurbished and refitted it with modern, forward-thinking elements to give it a second life as Steampunk. This recycling of history allows authors, costumers, designers, and more creative minds to select the best aspects of Victoriana—the romantic flavors, the aesthetics—while altering the history with some political corrections and improvements—especially

ABOVE

The Road to Atlantis by Maurice Grunbaum and Olivier Dreamkeeper. Photo by DECCO. With these bio-punk influenced costumes, Grunbaum envisions a great steam-powered civilization based on the fantastical island of Atlantis or the mythical lost continent, Mu. In this alternate vision that wanders far beyond the traditional Victorian milieu, recycled seashells are the basis for another kind of steam.

RIGHT

Steam Atlantis by Maurice Grunbaum. Photo by David Salou.

from a feminist and multicultural perspective. I see recycling in my costume art as a clear extension and integral part of the Steampunk directive."

Many designers find that their best pieces draw on something close to their heart. Likewise, design is often most interesting and innovative when it arises authentically from the experiences and cultural context of its maker.

To that end, costume designer Maurice Grunbaum urges the aspiring Steampunk to explore their own cultural heritage as they develop their personal look. Not only does this kind of exploration create fascinating and informative juxtapositions, it broadens the reach and definition of Steampunk itself. Grunbaum says, "When we think about the word 'Steampunk,' every Steamer has a subconscious image of an aesthetic based on the British Victorian era. It evokes mustachioed gentlemen, aristocrats with frock coats, dandies wearing exploration glasses on their top hats while flying their revolutionary dirigibles. . . . Alas, a lot of people tend to stick to that description and not explore any further."

But, he says, "the Victorian model is only one side of the multifaceted, vast, and rich Steampunk world. . . . To me, the richness of the Steampunk movement is its cultural diversity that spans way out of the ideological or political barriers set in the real nineteenth century. . . . What makes the movement so rich and vivid is its own capacity of perpetual renewal."

Architecture and Interior Design

Steampunk and retro-futurism have already made their collective mark on interior design, creating a look that can be easily categorized, and just as easily replicated. Though this look certainly hasn't reached the saturation point that one might term "cliché," it is fast becoming mainstream.

"The strong visual elements of the antique sciences and science fiction have never been seen in such abundance until Steampunk became popular," notes Art Donovan. "Antique maps, globes, orreries, clockwork mechanisms, nautical charts, and surveyor equipment have always been popular with decorators as antique additions to traditional homes and eclectic interiors. But in Steampunk, the unique, creative mash-up of vintage and contemporary devices is at the very core of the aesthetic and creative process."

The breadth of Steampunk's boundaries sets it apart from past movements in interior design. This flexibility can also have downsides, however. "As of 2013, Steampunk has been so firmly infused into architects' and designers' vocabularies that it's become an officially listed category on vintage merchant sites and in auction catalogs. This last part, however, is a double-edged sword because it allows merchants and dealers to call any antique industrial object 'Steampunk.' This inaccurate labeling is a marketing ploy used by sellers to attract a wider audience." Donovan argues that these items are not genuinely Steampunk—they are merely antique. They lack the whimsical or altered technological qualities that would distinguish them from basic Victoriana.

What does "authenticity" mean in terms of Steampunk? Perhaps the efforts of Steampunk art and design company ModVic, which strives to create a more authentic vernacular for the Steampunk interior, exemplifies one approach. ModVic is rooted in both the past *and* the future. As owner Bruce Rosenbaum explains, ModVic "repurposes and infuses modern technology into period antiques and salvage objects." The company's process involves hunting down "personal, meaningful objects, creatively combining them with relevant and cool period objects and machinery to transform the ordinary into incredible Steampunk functional art. The Steampunk art and design process celebrates history, while setting a path for a reimagined better future."

What does that better future hold? Steampunk is having at least one important effect on interior design and architecture as a whole: a renewed focus on craftsmanship, with a greater attention to detail. In recent decades, a lot of new construction has been overly focused on efficiency, cutting costs at the expense of quality. This type of approach had led to bland, monotonous, and shoddily constructed buildings: fast to build and affordable to buy, yet lacking the warmth and character of the construction of yesteryear. But people are longing once again for homes where every detail has been carefully planned, where each individual element has been made by a craftsperson who takes a real interest in the lasting quality of their work. As jewelry designer Friston comments on the Victorian age, "Artisans of that era were superb. Even a doorknob was designed with great skill and craftsmanship." It would be wonderful to see resurgence in built environments crafted with that same degree of attention and care.

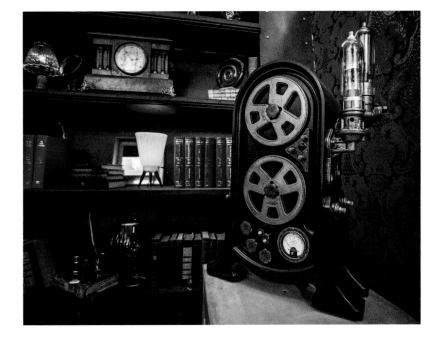

FINDING INSPIRATION

Tips from Designers

ABOVE
Gothic Dead Faery Skeleton Mini Top Hat by Amanda Scrivener

OPPOSITE ABOVE
Tamara, styled by Jessica Rowell. Modeled by Tamara Thompson. Photo by Michele LoBosco.

For our intrepid correspondents from the world of fashion and design, it seems that one beautiful thing often leads to another. Our interviewees spoke glowingly of the inspiration they find in the finer things in life, from rousing art to well-made objects to the grandeur of nature itself.

"I'm always inspired by anything visually stimulating! I love films with unique sets and costumes, especially if they incorporate an amazing story. My favorite directors are Wes Anderson, Julie Taymor, and Tim Burton. My favorite painters are Jenny Saville, Steven Assael, and Michael Hussar for the visceral way they portray human beings, and John Singer Sargent, John William Waterhouse, and the Pre-Raphaelite painters for their portrayal of fantastical stories and fabric. I love the JUXTAPOSITION of gritty realism *against* ethereal otherworldliness."

—*Kristin Costa*

"My wife Leslie's incredibly sharp sense of styling. Science fact and science fiction. The esoteric arts. Freemasonry. Ancient architecture. ARCHAEOLOGY and THE MYSTERIOUS, dimly lit corners of an old English library room *interrupted* by a single candle flame. All that—and a shop full of TOOLS and RAW MATERIALS. In my work, there is something elusive that I am always attempting to describe. I'm never fully satisfied. I'll keep working until I feel I've captured it. That 'it.' The thing that looks like the object in the center of the universe. Whatever the hell 'it' looks like. (I suspect it's spherical.)"

—*Art Donovan*

"A pattern of vintage braid on a Pinterest board, the color of a leaf in autumn or a cocktail in a book I happen to be reading, a late-night conversation or a visit to a museum. I try to **cram my life** full of wonderful things, and most of them rub off and filter down through **my brain** into a **weird new mix** that is UNIQUELY MINE. The main thing I need is time and space to work the ideas through." —*Jema Hewitt*

"I have always felt a connection to designers like Christian Lacroix and Alexander McQueen. The HAUTE COUTURE of the fashion world **inspires** me and keeps me designing the kinds of things that may be reserved for specialty now . . . but seen on the streets of the world in the future when we are no longer so self-conscious of what others think of us." —*Morrigana Townsend-Pehlke*

"BEAUTIFUL and **well-made** period objects and new, engaging technology. Ideas hit me with the full force of life itself. I see the past, present, and future merging all at once—like a time machine in my own mind. I'm motivated to push my art and design forward because it's what I love, what makes me feel good about getting up in the morning and making the day happen." —*Bruce Rosenbaum*

"I admire diverse forms of beauty and will seek inspiration in nature or from my surroundings. When realizing projects, I tend to **start with one element**. This could be a single sheet of fabric, an appliqué, or maybe even something as small as a button. It's then my objective to build upon or around the starting element, and sometimes it may end up subdued or hidden amongst what I've created around it. For each piece, the starting element is uniquely its own, and I'll continue to build upon a piece until I feel there's a sense of synergy." —*Jessica Rowell*

"**Museums**, historical places, **curios**, and stories inspire me. I really love creating, seeing the design take form, and the problem solving." —*Amanda Scrivener*

"Most of my work is inspired by one simple item, a vintage element or salvaged piece that begs a costume to grow organically around it. For example, the Steampunk Bird Hybrid idea grew from an earring that looked like the tip of a bird's talon. As the COSTUME *evolves* and develops, so does the story behind it." —*Paige Gardner Smith*

Steampunk Fashion and Design: A DIY State of Mind

Do you remember your first craft project? Maybe it was a dress or a skirt, labored over with scissors, needle, and thread. Perhaps it was a hand-painted lamp or a hand-stenciled border on a wall. Or possibly it was something for the garden: a handmade bench, a whimsical sculpture, or a well-crafted arch. Whatever it was, it was the sign of many greater things to come.

You're not alone. Many fashion and interior designers were first drawn to this type of work because they loved the feeling of working with their hands: the texture of fabric, paper, and paint; the Zen-like flow of deep concentration; and the immediate reward of a finished piece of work. (Even if the results aren't always quite as envisioned!) So it's no surprise that many continue to value the DIY approach and prize those hours in the studio where they can get back to basics and work with their hands once more.

Kristin Costa can certainly relate to this feeling. "I've always done everything myself," she says. "I feel like if I can't be a hands-on designer, then there's no point in designing, since the making of things is what makes me happy. Eventually, I may have to outsource, but the sample runs of each collection will always be made by me."

"DIY is essentially where my craft started," agrees fellow fashion designer Jessica Rowell. "As far back as I can remember, I have always altered my own clothes. . . . Long before I was designing, I used DIY as a method of self-expression. My art teacher used to tell me, 'One day we're going to have the class sketch you.' She truly thought I was a walking piece of art. When I eventually became a part of the cosplay scene, I learned to turn DIY into technique through years of trial and error. A lot of my works were extremely experimental in that sense."

Jema Hewitt's interest in clothing design also began developing when she was a young girl. "I always made my own clothes," she says. "My mother was an excellent seamstress, and I was a chubby little girl who couldn't ever find clothes that fit and had very distinct ideas of what they should look like." As the old saying goes, if you want something done right, do it yourself! And in fact, having a specific vision of something you'd like to have, with no idea where to get it except to make it with your own two hands, is wonderful motivation for learning new creative skills.

Paige Gardner Smith declares that "DIY is not only my method but my message as well." While Smith can manage the odd bit of hand-stitching, she says that sewing machines and patterns are more likely to give her a "cold sweat." So when she began planning her first Steampunk costume, she turned to some simple hacks and shortcuts to cut down on stitches. "Glue, safety pins, staples, grommets, and shoelaces took the place of sewing. To make up for my lack of metalworking and leather-riveting skills, I sought leather, plastic, and metal pieces with existing holes so I could hook or wire them together." Finding a way to assemble costumes *without* sewing is its own fun, unique challenge. And, Smith says, sharing these tips and tricks can be a good way to offer a down-to-earth welcome to aspiring costumers finding their way. "It's become my favorite pleasure to share the hacks and tricks I find with beginning costumers and those new to Steampunk DIY," she says. "It's fun to turn my fancy bustle upside down and show someone that it's actually a little girl's Easter dress that's flipped over and tied around my waist without a single stitch."

For interior designers, the DIY approach is equally important. For instance, Art Donovan lists some of the fields of expertise required for his practice: "In my lighting designs, of course I need some heavy rendering, wood, and metalworking abilities. Painting and finishing is also critical. That is, knowing the properties of every type of paint, dye, and pigment imaginable. Also, the skill of how to correctly fasten parts together. But there is nothing more important in my designs than the ability to predict the sequence of assembly. That's everything! Without the proper sequence for all the varied components, the piece simply can't be put together." When it comes right down to it, the work that designers do is often highly technical and firmly grounded in the nitty-gritty.

Of course, there are times when doing something *right* involves turning to the right people for expertise. As Bruce Rosenbaum says, "I'm not a mechanic or scientist. I employ lighting, electronic, digital, mechanical artists and engineers to design and fabricate our projects." And, as a matter of fact, architecture is the perfect example of a craft that requires serious expertise. At the moment, we can only point to a few Steampunk buildings; entire Steampunk cities exist only in the clouds and in the worlds of our imagination. But we can confidently say that, for tomorrow's retro-futurist architect, finding the right people to help create and construct her vision will be absolutely crucial. We're all about thinking big, and thinking big often requires a village. *Especially* when the task at hand is building one.

Fashion designer Morrigana Townsend-Pehlke gets to the heart of the matter: "I am lucky in that I have some amazing friends and family who know how to put together a working pair of goggles, carve a kraken walking cane, or create a set of wings that open and close on their own, and are willing to work with me to see one of my visions come to fruition."

TOP
Digital Grotesque (Gilding) by Michael Hansmeyer and Benjamin Dillenburger
BOTTOM
Digital Grotesque (Surface Coating) by Michael Hansmeyer and Benjamin Dillenburger. Photo by Demetris Shammas and Achilleas Xydis.

School for Steampunks: Mastering Hands-on Skills

ABOVE
Serpent Twins, created by
Jon Sarriugarte and Kyrsten
Mate, and their "Empire
of Dirt" crew. Design team
Because We Can assisted in
the fabrication and provided
additional support.

Now, creativity is the foundation of great design. But good ideas are just the beginning. To get the big results you're picturing, you may need to brush up on some hard skills, too . . . the practical techniques that enable designers to turn vision into reality. Sometimes this means starting from scratch, which can be scary—but it's well worth the risk.

"I have always been interested in how things work with nimble fingers," says Jema Hewitt, discussing the journey she took to master her craft. "So, from studying art and needlework at school I went on to learn skills like ceramics, silversmithing, and printmaking. . . . After the very basic techniques were learned, I asked lots of questions of other artists I admired, watched how they made things, and then tried them out myself later. Every job brought new challenges to work out, too. More research and different bits of knowledge get filed away over time."

Kristin Costa agrees. "I am constantly learning new skills, depending on what my projects call for. I just released an origami-themed collection in which I had to teach myself a number of origami techniques that I'd never done before, including making origami pieces out of six-foot lengths of canvas." Likewise, says Amanda Scrivener: "I sign up all the time to attend workshops by other artists to build on my skills."

Meanwhile, like many of our contributors to the chapter on art and making, Art Donovan learned many of his skills on the job, working in the toy industry in the 1970s. "It was like a marine boot camp for artists, because you used every art medium and art tool available: markers, oils, acrylics, gouache, pastels, pencil, tech pen, you name it. We learned how to sculpt in clay and high-density foam for prototypes. We used every kind of paper-and-cardboard folding method known. But the most important skill was knowing how to create a finished product *fast*!"

Donovan's comments illustrate one of those universally acknowledged truths about creative work: There's nothing that motivates a struggling artist like a looming deadline! If you're having trouble making progress in your artistic pursuits, sometimes a bit of external pressure can help. We recommend making a commitment to some outside party—and maybe even biting off just a bit more than you can reasonably chew.

If you're trying to flex your fashion muscles, look for outside commissions: You can offer to outfit a friend for a special occasion, or work with a local theater company on costuming. (They'll be grateful!) If it's interior design you're interested in, you could always rent a booth at a flea market or design an installation for an upcoming art show. As Donovan concludes: "In any career you plan to stay in, there are no wrong turns. Everything you do adds to your knowledge and skills."

Crafting a Rococopunk Jacket from Found Materials

by Megan Maude

Creating a richly layered outfit can be intimidating. It's easy to look at the amazing things other people are making and then to talk yourself out of doing anything before you even begin. How do they cram so many amazing intricacies into one garment? How can anything you come up with ever compare? Since I am lucky enough to have a boatload of talented friends, I have this problem all of the time. To combat the feelings of inadequacy, I like to find a point of inspiration to use as a center and then start collecting materials. I'm not always precisely sure where I'm headed until I get there, and I think that's okay. Sometimes I know precisely what I need, and other times I just have to start amassing supplies until I have a number of options to play with. That's what I did when I decided to make this Rococopunk redingote (which is just a fancy French way to say riding coat).

Rococopunk is a little different than Steampunk, because the punk comes from actual punk rock. It's a mash-up of the rococo era and old-school punk, where the two things are seamlessly combined and conveyed simultaneously. While Rococopunk isn't exactly a branch of Steampunk, it also wouldn't really exist without Steampunk's presence. It is at once mocking and complementing the movement.

The first time that my friends and I did a Rococopunk group, nobody else was doing it—anything we came up with was going to be interesting and original! However, by the next go-around we had a whole slew of new faces participating, and so I felt like I had to come up with something bigger and better than what everyone else would have. It was no longer enough to throw some vaguely rococo elements together with a punk flair and call it a day. This time, there was going to have to be some serious historical research, and it was going to have to come across in a totally new way. I was at a complete loss for where to begin until I found these fantastic floral tapestry Fluevog heels with a rococo silhouette. I knew that these shoes needed an ensemble to live up to their awesomeness!

I'm a huge history nerd, so I decided to loosely base my look on Marie Antoinette. Having a historical figure to loosely focus on gave me the opportunity to define a set of parameters to distort within. As it happens, Marie Antoinette was an avid horsewoman, much to the dismay of the court of Versailles. She rode astride like her male counterparts, and even had special riding pants made to match her redingotes, which was quite the controversy. In her day, bloomers hadn't even been invented, so imagine the scandal of full-on trousers! Marie went another step further, though, and had herself painted on horseback, which was a fashionable way for powerful men to convey their authority and military prowess. This served to at once show her dominance and also emasculate her husband, Louis XVI, who was already weak in the eyes of the public. How much more punk rock can a historical figure get? By the end of the eighteenth century, redingotes went from being purely utilitarian to being fashion statements, much like punk leather and denim

OPPOSITE
Rococopunk Jacket by Megan Maude. Styled and modeled by Megan Maude. Photo by Megan Maude.
BELOW
These floral heels inspired Megan Maude's look.

jackets did in the 1980s. Every punk needs a crazy jacket covered in studs, patches, and memories. So it was that I arrived at making a redingote to match my shoes.

1. Once I knew that I was going to make a redingote, I had to decide how to marry the historical garment with the iconic punk jacket. When you think of a punk jacket, either denim or leather comes immediately to mind, and so I settled on denim with a leather collar. Problematically, I wanted the classic denim jacket look to somehow shine through the historically based construction of the redingote. I didn't think normal denim yardage from the fabric store was going to cut it, so when I found these heinous pink denim jackets at a surplus store, I knew I had to find a way to use them.

2. Very carefully, I went about removing the flamingos and cutting the denim jackets apart into the largest sections I could manage, but none of the sections were big enough on their own to cut the redingote pattern pieces out properly. It turned out to be a good thing because it forced me to add another layer to the final design. I pieced the sections together to make larger, more usable pieces of fabric, and where I joined them, I used a dark red contrast stitch that was the same as the topstitching that I planned for the rest of the garment. Repurposing the found jackets into makeshift yardage allowed me to preserve the classic denim jacket details while adding more interest.

3, 4. Since the main fabric for the redingote was solid pink, I wanted to bring in more of the colors from the shoes with an interesting patterned fabric. At first, I had considered some type of plaid, but the world was not offering up anything that appealed to me. So, once again, I resorted to making my own solution. I found some lightweight denim yardage at a local fabric shop and decided to splatter-bleach it like punks so often do with their jeans. Then I overdyed the bleached fabric with teal Rit dye to make it a more desirable tone. Pro tip: To keep the dye from bleeding onto your other clothes or skin, wash the fabric with a cup of white vinegar.

5. I wanted to add some of the emblematic rococo-era ruffled trim along with decorative braid, so I made long strips, to be gathered into ruffles, of my manipulated fabric. In the late eighteenth century, clothes were made completely by hand, yet they were still covered with yards upon yards of ruffles. Finishing all of those edges with a rolled edge—like we would today—would have proved a Sisyphean task. Instead, they would simply pink the edges to keep them from fraying—they actually had special pinking irons that were used like stamps, made specifically for the purpose. A far faster modern method is to use a pinking rotary cutter to cut the strips evenly while pinking them at the same time.

6. Another great modern convenience is the ruffler foot. If your machine doesn't have an official ruffler foot available, there are generic ones that can

1.

2.

3.

4.

5.

6.

be found that will fit most any machine. Instead of hating yourself for having decided to gather endless yards of ruffles, you can get it done in a snap.

7, 8. I didn't want to just tack on modern punk patches and pins, so instead I created patches based on history. My favorite patch is one that exceptionally few people understand, which, I think, makes it killer. It's a picture of Christoph Willibald Ritter von Gluck, who was Marie Antoinette's childhood music teacher. In later life, she became his patron, even though it wasn't a very popular move on her part. In stencil-style letters over the image, the patch says, "Gluck you!" which is an obvious play on a slightly more offensive phrase. I find this endlessly amusing, even if not everyone will get it.

7.

8.

The Gluck patch was surprisingly easy to make. There are a whole host of ready-to-print fabrics on the market these days, including cotton, cotton twill, silk, and silk organza. When printed with an ink-jet printer and then heat-set, many of them become washable, and when the paper stabilizer backing is removed, they feel just like any other fabric. I used the printable silk to make the Gluck patch because I felt like Rococopunk should be kind of luxe.

That luxury, when mixed with the rougher aesthetic of punk, is ultimately what makes Rococopunk so effective. It creates a dichotomy within itself that provides extremely interesting, playful visuals. It was that visual lushness that drew artists such as Adam Ant to the look back in the 1980s, and it has remained relevant even today, albeit in a different way. Finding inspiration in Rococopunk is, at a glance, so easy, but when you get into the nuts and bolts, it can be overwhelming. It makes all the difference in the world to find that one point of inspiration and let it take you where it will!

....

Megan Maude is an independent designer and seamstress whose influential works in the fields of Gothic Lolita and Steampunk have been featured in many books and magazines dedicated to those aesthetics, including the *Gothic & Lolita Bible*, *Gothic Beauty Magazine*, *Anatomy of Steampunk*, and more. She is perhaps most well known for creating the Nerfpunk and Rococopunk styles.

From Pattern to Product: The Working Process

So you're probably wondering: After you've found your inspiration and locked down some solid skills, what happens next? For the working designer, what does the actual day-to-day process of creation look like? Here are some possibilities.

ABOVE
Punk Victorian by Paul Harvey

Fashion

Jessica Rowell typically starts by taking inventory in the studio; if she doesn't have on hand what she needs to begin a project, she goes shopping at fabric and thrift shops. "Sometimes I have a specific vision and other times my direction will develop organically while pairing textiles and notions together on the spot." This process is quite organic and intuitive. When inspiration strikes, she likes to get to work immediately; however, while some pieces can be completed within a couple of days, others may take months.

Paige Gardner Smith has a similar process, equally informed by the tactile inspiration of reclaimed objects. She says, "Typically, I will collect interesting fabric remnants, clothing, knickknacks, broken toys, et cetera, with no real intent—just picked because they're an odd or a cool-looking thing. I sort them into bins that I walk past every day in my basement. Each daily walk-by sparks thoughts and ideas about how parts can be used for a costume or prop. This process is constant and shifting, and encourages refinement of costuming projects and ideas long before the first effort is made to build it."

However, Jema Hewitt takes a more conceptual approach. "For a big showpiece like a museum costume, it usually begins with a concept such as 'gin bustle dress' and a sketch on the back of an envelope, or a few lines of memo text, which then sit in the back of my brain for a while. Slowly, it will grow into a more cohesive idea, and that can take days or months while I work on other things. Next, I do a more technical-style drawing, pulling in any research I've done and working out what materials I'm going to need. Often, the design will change as I get distracted by a more interesting object or material as I gather bits together."

"I'll usually sketch ideas for a few months, without making what I'm drawing, until I'm certain it is worth it," agrees Kristin Costa as she describes her process leading up to a show. "Then I'll start to make smaller pieces and start sourcing materials, and the collection starts coagulating into something more cohesive. . . . In the final few weeks, I'll make the majority of the samples, aided by coffee and three hours of sleep a night. Sometimes I have people who help me, but often times it is too fast-paced for me to want to explain the weird processes to anyone, and it is quicker for me to do it myself. The night before the show, I usually make the finale dress, because I have a bad habit of saving my favorite design for the last minute. Then the show happens. . . . Then I usually get sick for a week or two, since I'd been forgetting to eat and sleep in the three weeks up until the show. After that storm passes, I'm able to see what people are responding to the most, and edit the pieces that I will produce in bulk for my own personal shop, and facilitate the production of pieces that I have gotten orders for. If the orders are large, I may even call in a few sewing assistants, or outsource simpler designs."

We've been there. A good reminder for aspiring and experienced artists and artisans everywhere: It's easy to neglect ourselves when we're focused on our creative work, but taking care of yourself is an important part of the creative process, too. Sleep, food, and exercise are all very conducive to the creator's long-term health!

Interior Design

Like Jessica Rowell, lighting designer Tanya Clarke lets her eyes and hands guide her in the initial stages of a project, counting on intuition to draw her to the right materials. "Once I decide on what type of piece I want to build, I will wander around a scrap-metal yard and pull pieces that may work for, let's say, a base. For me this is often the most important component, as it must be able to have wires pass through it, a space for an electrical transformer, and the ability to drill or fit piping into it. The rest is like Legos: what fits with what. The shape begins to take form—sometimes similar to what I had in mind, often not at all. The less I think about it, the better. Next, I do the electrical work, and the hand-sculpted solid-glass drops are added in the final stage. I work in silence because that's the way I like it."

For Art Donovan, the work begins with a drawing. "I design two-dimensionally. Length and width only! My initial thumbnail sketches and concepts are flat drawings, rarely considering the depth or 3-D quality of the piece. With this approach I'm looking exclusively for a dramatic silhouette—that rhythmic gesture. That proportional and complementary geometry. Volume versus detail. The process is entirely emotional in the very early sketch stages. Then I go directly to raw wood and metal, using enlargements of my original thumbnail sketches. After that, the three-dimensional aspects of a piece present themselves on their own."

As a client-focused consultant with a business to run, Bruce Rosenbaum usually begins with a client sit-down. "I interview my clients to understand their personal or organizational history, what makes them unique now, and what type of functionality they are looking for in an art installation. Once we know what we would like to make, we find the personal or period objects that will act as physical reminders of what was and is important to them. We then find the artists, artisans, craftspeople, and technologists to make it come together. After approved drawings, we start to fabricate, using period objects, wood, metal, cloth, electronics, technology—whatever it takes to create incredible Steampunk art and design."

ABOVE
Shiva Mandala by Art Donovan

Just remember, however you begin, you may wind up somewhere else! Unconventional solutions are Rosenbaum's secret strategy. For surprisingly sticky problems, he suggests "pivoting." "There is always another way in," he says. "I gather up my mental forces and rethink (reimagine) how to get to the goal—in another way, maybe at another time and place. Resilience and perseverance are the keys to success for anything in life."

Seven Pieces of Advice for New Designers

1. "I try to NOT get *too attached* to what the outcome of my pieces will look like. A lot of my work is made with reclaimed pieces, and each piece has its quirk. If I can find a way to use those quirks to my benefit, as opposed to viewing it as an obstacle, then we're both better off."

—*Tanya Clarke*

2. "*Choose* one TECHNIQUE or craft to learn and **perfect** at a time. If you've never sewn before, it might seem terribly boring to make a waistcoat rather than that huge flouncy crinoline ball gown you've always wanted, but couture sewing skills take time to acquire. Just as athletes train their bodies, artists train their hands and eye equally as hard."

—*Jema Hewitt*

3. "I would say to **stay** within your **comfort** ZONE of techniques and aesthetics for a while. There's no need to rush into your 'masterpiece' when you haven't learned to walk yet. Copy other artists' work as much as possible to learn the rationale behind their form and the materials. The desire (along with the ability) to create more complex things will evolve naturally."

—*Art Donovan*

4. "Because I'm using very cheap or free materials, **costume-build mishaps are not usually deal breakers.** I consider mishaps as beta testing—smile! Curiously, I've found that my errors with paint, glue, and holes in the wrong place can sometimes lead to a better result in the end. Mistakes force the builder to think creatively, to discover unconventional solutions. I've also learned through experience which crafting materials make excellent bandages—for the more injurious mishaps that sometimes occur. My costume projects are not complete until they are christened with blood or tears, or both."

—*Paige Gardner Smith*

5. "The greatest advice I can give is to not abandon your passions, no matter what, and *never* COMPROMISE your integrity and authenticity."

—*Jessica Rowell*

6. "Start out small. *Find* a PERIOD OBJECT you love. Think not only what it was, but what it could be with some technological improvements and 'opposite thinking.'"

—*Bruce Rosenbaum*

7. "*Open* yourself up to the **possibility** that how it's 'usually' done . . . is not how you're going to **achieve** your **dreams.** If you love what you're doing . . . and you're willing to pour that love into your creation, then let it happen however it happens, even if it's not the 'norm.'"

—*Morrigana Townsend-Pehlke*

OPPOSITE

Zoetica by Jessica Rowell.
Modeled by Zoetica Ebb.
Photo by Tas Limur.

Steamarama: The RetroFuture Home of Yesterday and Tomorrow

by Bruce and Melanie Rosenbaum

Concept

RetroFuture House Exterior/Space

Style: Blend of high-style Queen Anne Victorian and Craftsman arts-and-craft design

Size: Two floors, approximately 3,000–4,000 square feet

The 1876 U.S. Centennial Exposition in Philadelphia was our country's first official world's fair and showed off the current inventions and technology of the period, along with how our homes and lives had changed in the previous one hundred years. The exposition was designed to show the world the United States' industrial strength, ingenuity, and innovative prowess.

At the exposition, a reconstruction of an early 1800s "colonial kitchen," along with a spinning wheel and costumed presenters, marked how far the United States had come, growing from an agriculture-based society to a "modern" industrial civilization. Now, looking back, it's quite amusing to see how wrong the organizers of the exposition were in predicting the future, and how technology can take unexpected turns to transform our lives.

RetroFuture House

In the truest sense of Steampunk's alternate history tradition, we ask the "What if?" What if the organizers of the 1876 Centennial Exposition who created the "Future House" got their predictions one hundred percent right? What would their future have looked like within the Victorian/Industrial Age aesthetic that was popular during the period? To answer that, we've dreamed up **Steamarama: The RetroFuture Home of Yesterday and Tomorrow**, which is a name play off the 1939 New York World's Fair exhibit, Futurama: The World of Tomorrow. This would be a fully immersive, interactive Steampunk exposition that shows what rooms in a Steampunk house would have looked like if the creators of the 1876 Centennial Exposition had predicted accurately what technologies and modern conveniences would have been integrated into our homes, fashion, and design—but within the Victorian and Industrial aesthetic of the period.

The majority of the objects would be authentic to the Victorian/Industrial period in one way or another and transformed by infusing modern technology functionality into the pieces.

RetroFuture House Interior: Technology, Rooms, and Objects
Possible Technologies Employed

Infrared (IR) multi-touch frames

Infrared camera. Used with projectors to create interactive surfaces that are non-LCD.

Rear-projection acrylic/film. Multiple products in this area are employed to create nonstandard interactive surfaces (irregular shapes, floating frames, etc.).

Semitransparent mirrored film (Mylar, Gila Privacy Film) for LCD mirrors. To employ hidden interactive control (capacitive systems, IR systems, vision systems).

IR pen. Modern pens with a classic look retrofitted to use IR LEDs as writing nubs.

Metal bar capacitance. Through the use of inlaid metal electrodes, capacitive controls can be added to wooden objects (inlays have a classic look while providing a modern function, and can be used for any switch type of behavior).

Leap motion. Used for hands-free interactions (motion and accurate hand-position tracking at a distance, and can be inlaid into furniture flush-mounted).

Kinect. Full-body motion capture that can be used to track motion between rooms and supply range-finding data.

LCD panels. For video content that can be hidden.

Pico projectors. Easy to hide, easier to fabricate with, and affordable laser projection for zero-focus installation.

Ultra/short-throw projectors. Super-short throw distance (distance from projector to projection target) for DLP or LCD for vivid picture quality.

Augmented reality/cast augmented reality. Allows for per-viewer stereoscopy. Can be used with any surface or object affixed with a retro-reflector. Can also be used to create visual overlays, menu systems, etc., and RetroFuture stereoscope.

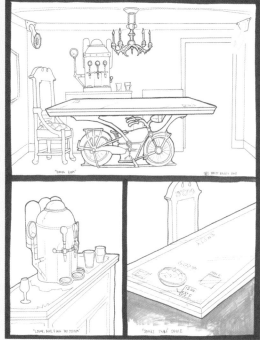

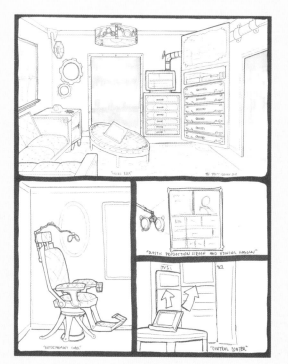

Foyer

Wedding time-capsule clock

Home personalized total sound systems (Music follows you from room to room!)

Fully armed Steampunk alarm system with aperture/camera door peephole

Internet access for guests and family

Dining and Entertaining Room

Dining table. Glass top with an Indian Motorcycle base. Tabletop is a "smart table" that informs guests of the menu and the times for finished preparation and serving of dinner items.

Serving table and bar with Steampunk beer-brewing system

Family, Living Room, and Home Theater

Central control station for all home theater components

Period dentist chair and dental equipment

Virtual reality game system

"KITCHEN"

"TOUCH SCREEN TABLE TOP"

"DIGITAL SEE-THROUGH REFRIGERATOR WITH INFO DISPLAY DOORS"

Kitchen

Constant sound and speaker system

iPad/house-control pod for charging

Wall-mounted, gear-shaped digital seasoning dispenser (Turn and input serving amount requested.)

Touch-screen countertop for island, used for the Internet, media, etc.

Digital touch-screen dials for oven and stovetop burners

Adjustable mood lighting

Digital side chef system (Input recipe and follow directions in real time.)

C-GPS (Culinary Gastro-Preparation System)

Window and digi-screen refrigerator and freezer system

Touch-system sink system and garbage disposal

Specially etched cityscape artwork over burner system (Steam simulates real Steampunk city!)

"OFFICE"   BRETT KELLEY 2012

"IN-DESK PRINTER/SCANNER"

"MEETING ROOM TABLE W/ DIGITAL WORK SPACE"

Office
Modified organ as computer workstation

Tri-screen tabletop

Submarine-themed lighting on ceiling and wall

Dock for home device

Plastic digital display screen, for calendar and time sheet/clock for work schedules

Snapshot camera turned into Skype camera for meetings

Sub-hatch for soundproofing room

Scanner/printer built into office desk

Cabinet of curiosities and records with panel tech glass that shows locations of documents

Meeting table with multiple chairs, modified tabletop touch screen for easy media demonstrations, and paperless note taking and scheduling

Floor rug with movable gears, covered by pane glass

Wall-mounted flat screen, once more for visuals and television viewing

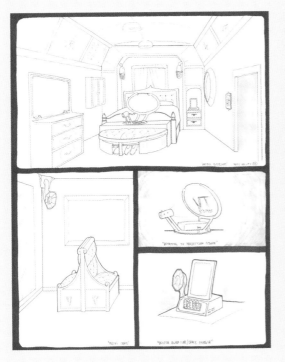

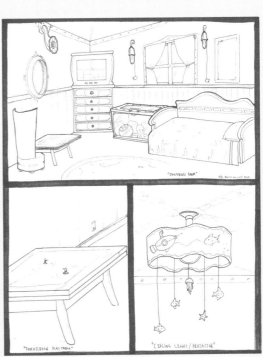

Master Bedroom
Pullman sleeping car bed
Accent wall, papered with Morgan Envelope
    factory postcards
Rotating projection screen for viewing content
    from different angles within the room
Bedside alarm clock and device changer

Baby's Room
Touch-screen play table
Ceiling light projector

....

Bruce Rosenbaum is a nationally acknowledged expert on Steampunk art and design. Rosenbaum's Steampunk art and design projects and that of his company, ModVic, have appeared in major media throughout the country, including the *Boston Globe*, the *Wall Street Journal*, and *Time* magazine, as well as on TV shows on Discovery, HGTV, MTV, TLC, and Boston's WCVB. He has been called the "Evangelist of Steampunk" by *Wired* magazine and travels the nation educating people on creative problem-solving techniques such as Janusian Thinking (combination and synthesis of opposites) and designing Steampunk objects, rooms, offices, hotels, clubs, and restaurants for his clients.

All images copyrighted by ModVic, LLC
Exterior and interior layout and floor plans by MLA Consultants
Room/object drawings by Brett Kelley

THE ENCYCLOPEDIA OF FANTASTIC VICTORIANA: ALTERNATIVE HISTORY EDITION.

READE HOUSE. The story of the Reade House is well known by now. Located in San Jose, California, the Reade House was the home of wealthy steam-robots manufacturer Frank Reade, his wife Mary, and their son Frank, Jr. The sudden death in 1883 of Frank and Frank Jr. plunged Mary Reade into a profound depression which was only dispelled by the words of a spirit medium, that "If our house had not been finished, I would still be with you. I urge you now to build a home, but never let it be finished—the sound of the hammers must never stop—for then you will live." In 1884 Mary started work on a house that would never stop being built—it would build itself. The house incorporated all of the most current technology of the Reade steam-robots and was programmed to never stop adding to itself. And it continues to do so today, spreading across suburban San Jose.

The Reade House is an impressive edifice. But apart from the famous van der Rohe/Le Corbusier exchange of the late 1930s there has been little written about the Reade House as art, as an aesthetic construct.

Walking around the house, one is first struck by the contrast between the exterior of the house—detailed, apparently finished, and serene—and its turbulent surroundings. The house is a poor fit for the neighborhood. The house is bracketed by barricades, stone walls which mark the line of demarcation beyond which the house will (supposedly) not be allowed to expand. Between the house and the federal barricades are the ruin of Highway 280 and the parking lots and tract houses which the Reade House's underground drill bits are consuming. On the other side of the federal barricades, Reade House is surrounded by sinkholes and a suburban San Jose neighborhood of mid-century houses long since abandoned. The population of San Jose has no confidence in the barricades and does not live in the neighborhood. Supposedly the Reade House's growth is slowing, and the owners speak of a downward rather than outward expansion of the Reade House. But no one wants to live too near the house.

Yet the house and neighborhood are, perhaps, not so ill-fitted as all that. The Reade House does not exist in isolation, despite the presence of the barricades. The house's burrowing machinery are notorious for causing localized "quakes" across San Jose, but supposedly the machinery avoids disrupting those houses which were built during the "New Gothic Revival" of the 1980s. In the larger context of the city the Reade House is not ridiculous, but a precursor of what is to come: the Reade House is the neighborhood's editor, transforming its surroundings.

In bright light, the exterior is that of an irregularly spaced late-Victorian home, sprawling in every direction: redwood, stained glass, the occasional Gothic Revival wing or Neoclassical segment. In bright light, it seems obvious that, on the "skin building" verses "muscle building" scale, the Reade House is as much a skin building as a muscle building.

But such a clear viewing is rare. More often the house is encased in smudgy coal smoke emitting from one of the many antennae-like chimneys, just as there is a constant smell of grease and soot about the Reade House and an endless low clanking, whirring, and grinding of machinery. At such times most of the house is obscured, and what is visible are the interior lights from the house's mechanisms—the propulsion for the sliding rooms, the elevator shafts, the corkscrewing spiral staircases—which obscure the wood veneer. In the dark, the Reade House's skin disappears, leaving only its muscles, sinews, and bones to be seen.

Those notorious shifting rooms have long defied architectural critics. As Le Corbusier said, "A house is a machine for living in, but it should not be a machine. The masterly, correct play of masses brought together in light has little to do with ambiguous, randomly rotating rooms in the shapes of flattened and off-kilter cubes, cones, spheres, cylinders and pyramids." One cannot discuss how well the architectural plan works with the building when the building is altered on a continual basis.

Also, in the dark it is possible to believe that more than just interior rooms are being constructed and shifted; that the outline of the house itself changes according to some internal master plan; that overnight towers sink, wings are dismantled, and gables flattened and used as floors; that the jutting out of the gables, windows, chimneys, and portes cochere are *deliberately* designed to obscure views and foul sightlines; and that the rumors are true, of entire floors filled with punch cards, following Mary Reade's supposed indoctrination in the ways of the "New Aeon of Dimensional Thought" of Charles Hinton and Aleister Crowley.

In fact, a look at pictures of the house over the years does hint at an internal harmony, and the order of the rooms being assembled speaks to some variation of the Fibonacci Sequence.

The architectural scheme of the building is supposed to bring daylight in, but only to the outer layer of rooms. The interior rooms are designed for dim light, via interior windows and crooked skylights, or bright lights, via the outsized fireplaces or the stained glass floors or ceilings, or even more unusual lighting, as with the imitation Amber Room. The rooms themselves are erratic in design: claustrophobic, often impressionistic, with a certain detectible loathing for right angles and straight lines.

In fact, the building begs the classic architecture school question: Who is it being built for? Its absence of lavatories; its emphasis on hallways which curve relentlessly and always seem to lead out rather than in; its stairways which lead nowhere; its uneven levels—the building does not evoke emotions so much as puzzlement. Was this Mary Reade's intention? The Reade House is architecture of aggression, not passivity, and ambition, not resignation—but whose aggression, and whose ambition?

Jess Nevins

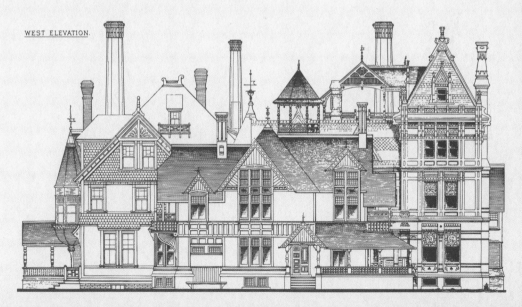

WEST ELEVATION.

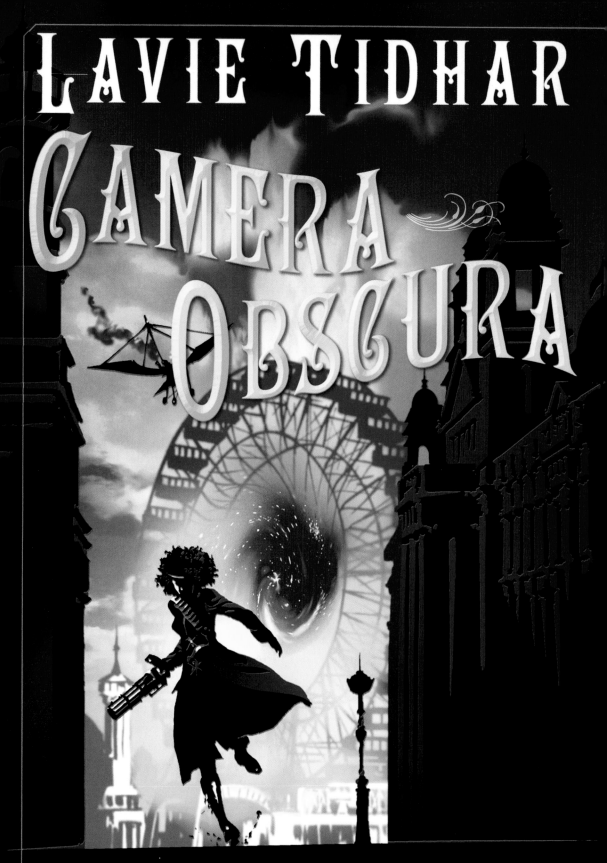

LAVIE TIDHAR

CAMERA OBSCURA

"A delight, crammed with gorgeous period detail,
seat-of-the-pants adventure and fabulous set-pieces."
THE GUARDIAN

STEAMPUNK STORYTELLING

Should fiction be used to address social and political issues? Is a powerful message more important than a good story, or vice versa? Is it even possible to tell a story that is not informed by some kind of ideological bent or bias? And how do you balance the need for accuracy and specific detail with having fun in your fiction? These are some of the questions being grappled with in different ways by the next generation of Steampunk storytellers, and in this chapter, they share a few of their answers and ideas. (For more writing advice from a fantastical and science-fictional point of view, we recommend *Wonderbook: The Illustrated Guide to Creating Imaginative Fiction*.)

Some storytellers turn to novels, others to short stories, some to plays—even bringing their narratives to the silver screen. And today, Steampunk storytellers are also exploring cutting-edge visual and interactive media like graphic novels or role-playing games. Regardless of the medium, the Steampunk storyteller's tradition is a long one; as documented in our prior volume, *The Steampunk Bible*, Steampunk began, first and foremost, with *stories*.

Some trace Steampunk's roots all the way back to the literature of the late nineteenth century: the novels of H. G. Wells and Jules Verne, and boys' adventure novels or "Edisonades." Others point to the 1980s novels of James Blaylock, K. W. Jeter, and Tim Powers, or William Gibson and Bruce Sterling's *The Difference Engine*. Either way, it was through the power of narrative that these retro-futuristic worlds first came to life, eventually giving rise to a creative and aesthetic movement spanning art, architecture, music, fashion, and dramatic performance.

This wasn't just escapist literature, even from the start—Michael Moorcock's *The Warlord of the Air* is a searing indictment of imperialism. As author Lavie Tidhar says, "I think Steampunk first emerged out of two things: the fun and the attraction of classic Victorian literature, from Sherlock Holmes to Jules Verne on the one hand, and from an awareness of just how horrible the Victorian era actually was. It's no surprise that the original Steampunks like Jeter found their inspiration in Henry Mayhew's *London Labour and the London Poor*, which documented the appalling conditions in the capital."

It is true, however, that not until recent years did Steampunk fiction become not just more commercial, but also, at times, more complex and diverse, with plenty of interesting cross-pollinations between genres. Today's Steampunk storytellers are spinning tales influenced by the fashion of cutting-edge cosplayers, the machines of makers like Jake von Slatt, and creating worlds set to the soundtrack of Victorian-influenced songsters. Some of it might be escapist, but some of it is transformational.

Thus the subgenre came full circle, picking up lots of nuance and complexity along the way. This might make Steampunk sometimes seem a little bit meta in its references. Yet, at its heart, Steampunk is also very old-fashioned in its approach to storytelling. In this aspect, although it may feel nothing like the heroic fantasy it has begun to supplant, it is actually very similar.

As author Tobias Buckell explains, "[Someone once] pointed out that, to writers (and their readers) in the early 1900s, farmland and preindustrial landscapes felt like the domain of a simpler, more understandable time. And that, to writers of the early 2000s, the early Industrial Age feels like the domain of a simpler, more understandable time as we hit an age of accelerating change. Steam and clockwork seem more understandable. It's a sort of technological Overton Window, if you want to be a bit precocious about it. So, to that extent, Steampunk is of a lineage of the same activity that spun out Tolkien, C. S. Lewis, et al. Fantasy, in many ways, is the use of the symbols and mythology of a previous age, reinterpreted for modern writers to examine the world around them (Tolkien to process World War One, for example). So much of genre work is just a mirror used to examine what already exists."

Brazilian writer Jacques Barcia also draws the connection to Tolkien, saying, "Just like 'medieval fantasy' has a huge number of fans—and I'm thinking about medieval fairs, Crusades reenactors and, yeah, Tolkien fans—Steampunks seem to be interested in that dreamland, that play, that game in which they're part of a world that looked so cool back in the day."

Writer and performer Anna Chen praises Steampunk for its imaginative potential, but from a different perspective. "Being half Chinese and half English, I straddle two major cultures," she says. "Steampunk has enabled me to grasp my history in a profound way while opening up all sorts of subversive possibilities. It gives shape to a lot of amorphous ideas I'd had over the years, about identity, imperialism, politics, race, philosophy . . . but with such a sense of adventure and excitement. It's like threading pearls."

On the technology side, Lev Rosen, author of the well-received debut *All Men of Genius*, believes that Steampunk allows us to work out our own anxieties, using the lens of the past. "I think we're at a point in history where technology is advancing at crazy speeds. We're being flung into the future really quickly, and that's intimidating, because we don't know what's coming. Every new piece of tech that comes out, from the Hadron Collider that people thought was going to cause a black hole to Google Glass, which people fear will be constantly taping and uploading every moment of life, brings these murmurs of anxiety. But if you take that tech and you put it in a fantastical, mad-science past . . . it becomes a way to interact with the ideas of advancing technology without being afraid of them. And I think that with us moving forward so quickly, a lot of people want to hold on to the past, too—there's a fear we could lose the past altogether, that e-books will somehow cause all paper books in the world to burst into flame. Steampunk lets us hold on to that past while still moving forward."

Whether you find that good or bad, it provides a clear example of how flexible Steampunk can be: utopian or dystopian, contained within the same scenario depending on context and point of view. This is the main reason Steampunk has vitality: It creates the argument for the progressive and the repressive within the same book, sometimes the same scenes. By bringing forward not just the positive idea of technological progress but all of the costs and terrible aspects that have their origins in the Industrial Revolution, it invites discussion and argument.

To others, like fiction writer, poet, and book reviewer Amal El-Mohtar, there's an essential issue that may be getting lost in the fascination with the "bling" of Steampunk.

"I submit," she wrote in a Tor.com post later reprinted in the anthology *Steampunk Revolution*, edited by Ann VanderMeer, "that the insistence on Victoriana in Steampunk is akin to insisting on castles and European dragons in fantasy; limiting, and rather missing the point. It confuses cause and consequence, because it is fantasy that shapes the dragon, not the dragon that shapes the fantasy. I want the cogs and copper to be acknowledged as products, not producers, of Steampunk, and to unpack all the possibilities within it."

What else would she like to see? "I want to see Ibn Battuta offered passage across the Red Sea in a solar-powered flying machine of fourteenth-century invention, and for that to be called Steampunk. . . . I want to see Steampunk where the Occident is figured as the mysterious, slightly primitive space of plot-ridden possibility. I want Steampunk divorced from the necessity of steam."

As you'll see, Steampunk is opening up to a wealth of new influences—it is, in fact, evolving into something that might be only half-recognizable to Verne or Wells, a fact they themselves might applaud.

Finding the Path to Steampunk

What makes a Steampunk storyteller? Not surprisingly, the wordsmiths we spoke to pointed to the literary works that influenced them most, listing dozens of books they had read as young adults and developing writers; these aesthetic stimuli proved a potent creative brew, inspiring some of our favorite stories in recent years.

"My favorite thing to read has always been nonfiction about history and other cultures," says Jaclyn Dolamore, author of *Magic Under Glass*. "Basically, what people are doing and have done, everywhere, any time. Of course, I also loved fiction, and the things you love when you're a kid imprint you forever. I have always loved the simple yet effective language and identifiable characters in children's literature like the Little House books, Betsy-Tacy, and L. M. Montgomery."

Diana Pho, founder of the popular Steampunk blog *Beyond Victoriana*, also points to her teenage reading habits. "My obsession with nineteenth-century literature started in high school with my passion for Jane Austen and the Brontë sisters, and my love for sci-fi has gone on much longer than that (I remember my first chapter books being the illustrated versions of *Twenty Thousand Leagues Under the Sea* and *Journey to the Center of the Earth*)." For Pho, Steampunk "is best expressed through writing and through performance," so the act of storytelling extends to the stage. Through her steamsona, she can explore her interests in history and culture, with a generous dose of imaginative play: "fantastical props, costume, and acting over-the-top."

Jedediah Berry is the author of *The Manual of Detection*, a retro-futurist fantasy that draws heavily on the aesthetic of 1920s noir. Berry's influences range from retro to contemporary. "The book was published around the same time as Jeff VanderMeer's *Finch* and China Miéville's *The City and the City*, both of which also play with the tropes of hard-boiled crime fiction," Berry comments. "Miéville suggested to me that we push for the term 'noird' ('noir' plus 'weird'), which I quite like, because it gets at many of my influences. They ranged, for that book, from classic hard-boiled writers like Raymond Chandler and Dashiell Hammett to authors of stranger stuff: Franz Kafka, Mervyn Peake, Angela Carter, and others."

"I'm an influence sponge," says Jacques Barcia. "I'm interested in a wide number of topics, and I'm really passionate about many of them: martial arts, the punk subculture, extreme metal, extreme left-wing politics, art, body modification. Poetry. Role-playing games. Everything and everyone is an influence, really. Dalí, Picasso, and Banksy. Anonymous, Jello Biafra, and Henry Rollins. Napalm Death, Nasum, and taiko. Bash and Paulo Leminski. Cory Doctorow and Subcomandante Marcos."

BELOW
Jedediah Berry. Photo by Lucy Hamblin.
BOTTOM
The Manual of Detection by Jedediah Berry (Penguin Press, 2009). Cover by Meighan Cavanaugh.

ABOVE

John Picacio's original cover art for *The Encyclopedia of Fantastic
Victoriana* by Jess Nevins (MonkeyBrain, 2005). This work
inspired the fanciful *Encyclopedia Victoriana* entries written as
original pieces by Nevins for this volume, located between chapters
and stunningly illustrated by John Coulthart.

Speculative fiction writer Nisi Shawl also spoke to us about her inspirations for her current novel-in-progress, *Everfair*, a Steampunk story set in the Belgian Congo. The novel is the result of influences ranging from the literary to the historical. "I'd been fantasizing for years about writing a novel featuring characters based on a certain group of historical personages: E. Nesbit, Colette, J. M. Barrie, George Bernard Shaw, H. G. Wells. I read about them, noticed certain correspondences in their lives and ways they might fit together."

Steampunk seemed like a natural fit for these interests, but Shawl found herself ambivalent about the genre. "I adored Victorian literature, I had this thing for heavy equipment—but it was the colonialist, imperialist subtext that repulsed me." Then a nonfiction book set in the time period—*King Leopold's Ghost* by Adam Hochschild—gave her the spark of inspiration that brought it all together. "That was the moment when the novel's inspirational ideas formed their proper constellation and I knew how I'd do what needed to be done."

Maurice Broaddus, who gave the anthology *Steamfunk* its name, also came to Steampunk through the lens of critique, with his desire to interrogate flawed assumptions leading to an intriguing and original work.

"I didn't know a lot about Steampunk in the beginning," he says. "I knew enough to make this joke on Twitter: 'I'm going to write a Steampunk story with all black characters and call it "Pimp My Airship."' It was after several editors wrote me to send it to them that I seriously explored the genre. I picked up *Extraordinary Engines* and the first of the VanderMeers' Steampunk anthologies. The stories were excellent, but something about them left me overall dissatisfied. It's like I was purposely excluded from a party. There was nothing culturally where I could see myself. Nothing. In fact, it almost seemed like a genre that purposely set out to not have to deal with, to put it delicately, any of the legacies of the society it harkens back to. And I said to myself, 'I can't do this,' because I could not see any 'me' in this universe. So I put on some James Brown, X Clan, and Public Enemy and began writing. It began as parody, but in a lot of ways, it was more protest."

For some, too, Steampunk fiction is simply a convenient shorthand for a creative vision they've been developing for some time, not to mention a much welcome community for those whose diverse and unusual interests had pushed them a bit off the beaten path.

Suna Dasi, the founder of *Steampunk India*, tells us, "I am one of those people who, after a lifetime passion for all things Victorian; a lifetime love of the macabre; of alternative ways of living and thinking outside the box, not to mention a taste for vintage sci-fi, were searching for community. Well, we all suddenly looked up to find the world had conveniently lumped the whole shebang into one genre that encompassed all of the above!"

One thing did trouble Dasi, however: the lack of complex, interesting Indian characters in Steampunk, particularly Indian women. Eventually, the issue became too pressing for her to ignore. She asked herself, "If it matters that much to me, why not have a crack at it myself? I wanted to create a world where the issues I'm addressing, if I am able, are not the main issue, but part of the tapestry. That took a while, and much research into Victorian India, Indian folklore, Indian heroes from history, Indian female warriors, and so on."

BELOW
Étienne Barillier and Arthur Morgan. Photo by ActuSF.
BOTTOM
Le Guide Steampunk by Étienne Barillier and Arthur Morgan. Cover designed by Alexandre Bourgois.

Dasi's own background demonstrates that the impulse to tell these stories is personal; her heritage has exerted an "enormous and vital influence" on her desire to write Steampunk specifically. "My ancestors left India around 1860, on a British East India ship from Madras, bound for the Caribbean as indentured workers—little more than slaves. My grandfather was born on a coconut plantation in Saint Vincent and raised Hindu. He was eventually released from his born status and married a native girl from Aruba in the Dutch Caribbean. My mother left for the Netherlands, where I was born and raised. Indian, Dutch, and English maritime history, women's history, and the Industrial Revolution have always held a particular sway over my imagination, and Steampunk provides me with the most elegantly fitting mold for writing that unifies all of them."

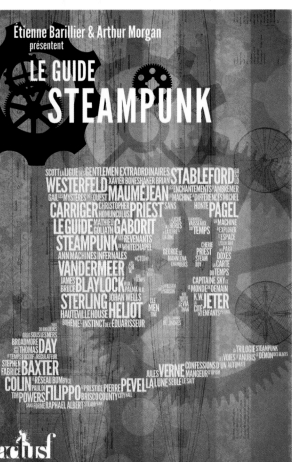

French author Arthur Morgan was also drawn to Steampunk for its weird amalgam of history and fantasy—and truth that is sometimes stranger than fiction. "What fascinates me with the Victorian era, and definitely got me into Steampunk, is the strange mix of industrial positivism, science, technology and fables, superstition, the supernatural. I love the rationalization of nonrational disciplines like spiritism and ether. So I came to Steampunk through literature—*Dracula, The Strange Case of Dr. Jekyll and Mr. Hyde*—and through comic books. . . . My favorite characteristic is the meta-reference of Steampunk literature. It mixes historical and literary references, which makes it intellectually mind-blowing."

Morgan's colleague Étienne Barillier echoes Dasi's take: "Steampunk was around long before K. W. Jeter coined its name," he says. "Most people who actually love Steampunk loved it before they even discovered the name. . . . I've never met a French person my age who doesn't remember watching *Wild Wild West* as a kid. You know H. G. Wells, Jules Verne, even if you never read their books. You know them because they belong to your culture, the very same culture Steampunk is building itself upon. Explaining Steampunk to your grandma is easy!"

Because Steampunk is a broad church, it tends to cannibalize works that aren't necessarily Steampunk. For example, China Miéville doesn't think of his Bas-Lag novels (*Perdido Street Station*, *The Scar*, *Iron Council*) as Steampunk, and yet a certain level of technology on display in those books means that some readers do use that label to describe Miéville's work.

Paolo Bacigalupi, author of the best-selling *The Windup Girl*, describes a similar experience. *The Windup Girl* had been out for a while when reviewers began describing it as Steampunk. "Honestly, I was perfectly happy to have it adopted, because if someone sees something they like in one of my books, then I'm happy they're happy," he says. "But I never thought of it as Steampunk when I was writing it.

"In my mind, Steampunk feels nostalgic. It's a looking back to a history that's cooler and more intricate and fetishized than our own true past. Fundamentally, it seems to me to be an exploration of fantastical histories that never were, but would have been wild and wonderful if they just could have been. So while *The Windup Girl* has dirigibles and intricate muscle-powered engines, at its root, it's explicitly not about an alternate past. It is intended as an extrapolation into the future, and as a prod for readers to consider our present moment. It's very specifically about now, and where we're headed from here. My sense is that this isn't Steampunk's prime directive."

It's clear that Steampunk has the ability to address big, complex issues. Has it realized that potential yet? It might have started to.

As author Richard E. Preston notes, "Steampunk's pretty, and that always has appeal. But Steampunk is also laden with vast potential to explore the modern world, and people are beginning to recognize its power as allegory. The Victorian/Edwardian era (Steampunk embraces this period, and also roughly extends back into the late eighteenth century and forward to the end of the Great War) was a time of immense progress, darkness, and contradiction. Most of its conflicts are still with us today: man versus machine, economic progress/empire versus exploitation/colonialism, industrialization versus nature, hedonism versus sexual repression, sexism versus female suffrage and equality, Darwinism versus creationism, utopianism versus disillusionment, and on and on. A writer can really tackle our modern life through Steampunk, and I think readers will continue to respond to that. . . . The *great* Steampunk novel has yet to be written."

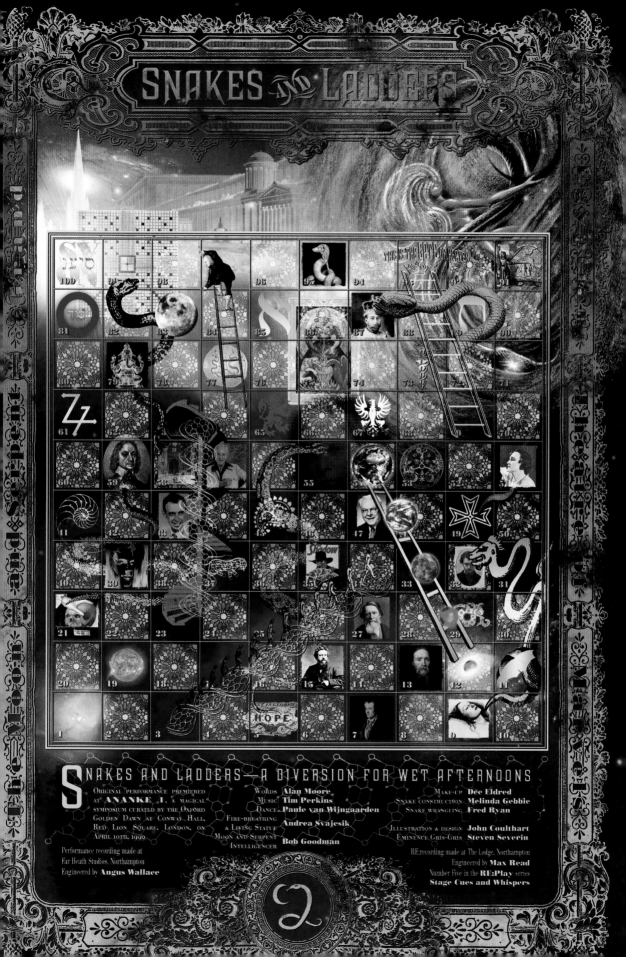

. . . .

Steering Clear of Clichés and Pursuing the New

For Steampunk storytellers, steering clear of clichés is less about the visual aesthetic of goggles and gears—though that does play a role—and more about the kinds of stories being told. The characters we encounter, the adventures they experience, the environments they inhabit, and the conflicts they endure. Like Suna Dasi, who set out to tell the stories she wanted to hear, an aspiring Steampunk storyteller should dig beyond the surface and search for what's original.

"I think typical prim and proper Victorian society has been done to death at this point," comments Jaclyn Dolamore. "The Victorian era is probably my favorite historical period, I just want it out of the box a bit. I always like seeing more diversity of time periods and places."

Airship pirates, another tried-and-true staple of the genre, may also have become overly cliché. "Airship. Pirates. Have. To. Go," declares Diana Pho. "Mostly because they are a glorification of a criminal subculture without a thorough examination of what real pirate life was like, or how creative a speculative look at pirate life could be. And because most situations that involve airship pirates in fiction have become uninspired and predictable."

But while some might feel that the swashbuckling stratospheric airship has sailed, others are still having plenty of fun with the concept, and finding new ways to repurpose the trope. As Richard E. Preston notes, "My Pneu-

OPPOSITE AND ABOVE
Plnou Parou, a Czech
Steampunk anthology edited
by Martin Šust. Cover art by
Pavel Trávníček.

matic Zeppelin series is written for a reader who has never experienced Steampunk before. I sort of grabbed the clichés — the zeppelin, the goggles, the Victorian clothing — and ran with them to tell the story of a crew of a ship at war. I picked Steampunk because I wanted to write a swashbuckling tale with strong female characters, some in positions of command. I also have zebra-striped aliens involved. Steampunk is fun. It has a lot of Edgar Rice Burroughs and Henry Rider Haggard at its core." Those strong female characters might just be the key, though — along with several other characters, including the airship's captain, who are thoroughly kind and decent people. Steampunk without cynicism might be just as refreshing as finding different tropes through which to showcase it.

Lev Rosen calls out what he sees as another tired plot mechanism: overused Lovecraft lore. "There is one trend I've been noticing and having some trouble with of late — this tendency to throw Lovecraftian monsters in without any rhyme or reason. They come at the end of the book, usually, where it's revealed that the evil scientists/cabal/whatever wasn't just killing people to further his experiments/take over the world/whatever but also because he was opening a portal to a realm beyond ours where creatures beyond our imagination lurk. And then they come pouring out and start destroying stuff, and then the heroes stop them. I like a Lovecraftian terror as much as the next guy, but they always seem tacked on at the end — no hint of their existence before they appear — and then they always die so easily."

Rosen also cites as clichés the Queen's Secret Agent and the Detective and His Assistant (with a special tip of the hat to Dr. Watson and

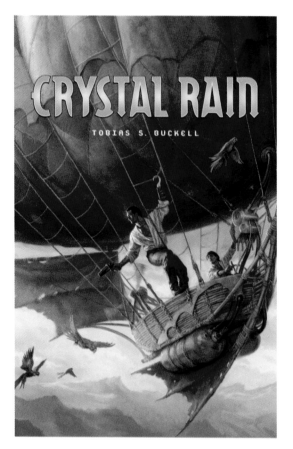

Sherlock Holmes). However—and this is a big however—what falls flat for one person may feel totally fresh to another, especially with the right twist. "In all fairness, though," Rosen admits, "a lot of the stuff I used in *All Men of Genius* has gotten pretty stale by now, too; spunky girl scientists; evil, clawed robots; London-based—you see it a lot. I'd like to see more queerness in Steampunk, more people of color, more people who aren't Christians or atheists (and who actually interact with their beliefs); more Steampunk that takes place in countries other than the U.S. and Britain."

Tobias Buckell points to this desire as well, saying: "I'm trying to have a conversation with a larger world. But I'm also trying to write these books that I would have killed to have had when I was out there back in the beginning, reading and not finding people who were like me: living in a diverse world, or of a diverse background themselves."

Jacques Barcia says, "I think this is changing now, but most Steampunk authors and fans seem to forget that, behind the wonders, exciting discoveries, and romanticism, the Victorian era was marked by imperialism, genocide, wars, and deforestation. It was high chimneys and black smoke. It was men, women, and children working eighteen-hour shifts, feeding the fires of 'progress,' digging in coal mines. But it was also a time of revolutions. The First International, the Paris Commune. The rise of feminism. Independence wars around the world. That's what interests me in Steampunk. The wondrous life of the poor, the outsider, the colonized, in a world populated by clockwork automatons, Crowleyan magic, and social struggle. I think this is a cliché, but I'd love to see more punk in Steampunk."

For imaginative authors such as Tobias Buckell, the story and the setting go hand in hand to give readers a taste of a much wider world. "I was trying to create a Steampunk adventure that explored some of those issues with helpings of action and adventure, while also hoping to bring a bit of complexity to it," he says. "By using the Caribbean peoples, by exploring the issues of conquest and war, I was hoping to maybe chart a course for getting the best of both worlds. The aesthetic fun of Steampunk geared in with a diverse cast."

Suna Dasi also plays with characters and setting, pursuing her original goal of creating stories where women could claim the spotlight as heroines, while not losing sight of the big picture: Steampunk should be fun. "I tend to put women in unusual settings or places and try to think through, in as much detail as possible, how these situations would pan out. . . . In the grand tradition of fiction and workshop tinkering, I am warping, bending, and altering things, but in my Steampunk India you will still find nasty British ruling classes and nasty patriarchal Indian mores alongside some morally liberated characters. However, the political correctness can kill creativity, so I'm careful in its use. I am not on a crusade to excuse, elevate, or exonerate either the British or the Indian nation for anything. That said, there is still plenty of room left for general sociopolitical observation, satire, and gender politics without becoming an apple-crate preacher. . . . There needs to be enjoyment in the process, and this can be achieved without losing either integrity or amusement. I need to have fun."

Some, however, find the process of provocation and challenge to be the most interesting part of the work. Nisi Shawl is structuring her approach around asking questions, first and foremost. "I see mostly the same clichés in Steampunk as I do in other imaginative literatures: the unmarked state (white, cis, able-bodied, et cetera) is the same, and non-European cultures are a sort of spice to the stories rather than their essence. There is a Boys' Own Adventure tone to the narratives I've read, which I find really problematic, even when they're somewhat subverted by giving the narrative voice to a girl or a woman. . . . Mere gender switch-ups do not erase colonialist imperatives." But, as Shawl says, "That weakness can also be a strength if the givens are questioned. Then the questions the author needs to ask are right there, right at hand."

Lavie Tidhar points to addressing those issues up front: "What I enjoyed doing in the Bookman Histories—and it's in the context that we have these aliens, essentially—is that a lot of the technology may appear to be impossible Victorian but can actually be described in terms of present-day science fiction. I liked that. That is, for the characters, the technology can only be described in nineteenth-century terms, but for the reader, we can sort of see how this is post-2000 SF dressed up. I also hope the books allowed me, in however light a way, to discuss issues of colonialism, and also, since this is a book of alternate history, to try and imagine how the nineteenth century could have been better—hence the limited European settlement in America, limited colonialism in Africa, more freedom for women, less obvious racism (and both the heroes of *The Bookman* and *Camera Obscura* are not white, without that necessarily defining them)."

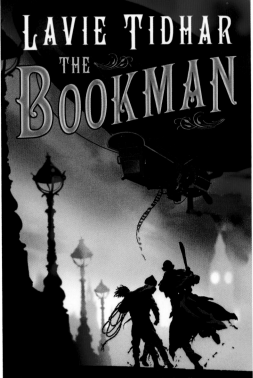

"A stunningly imaginative remix of history, technology, literature, and Victorian adventure that's impossible to put down... simply the best book I've read in a long time." — JAMES P. BLAYLOCK

OPPOSITE ABOVE
Crystal Rain by Tobias S. Buckell (Tor Books, 2006). Cover art by Todd Lockwood.
OPPOSITE BELOW
Jacques Barcia. Photo by Ivson Miranda/Itaú Cultural.
ABOVE
The Bookman by Lavie Tidhar. Art by David Frankland.
OVERLEAF
Kraken vs. Airship: Battle Scene. Concept by Richard Ellis Preston Jr. Art by Jeremy Zerfoss.

4 Reinforcements (Sabrina arrives with musket team, ineffective musket volley, crewman Valentine wounded, grappling cannon fired)

Advantage, Beastie (kraken forms tentacle wall, fighting retreat, Steinway killed) **3**

Battle Begins (Buckle's bow ice team engages, crewman Hudson killed, stern ice team rescued) **2**

Latching On (Kraken attaches to airship, stern ice team trapped) **1**

Kraken vs. Airship: Battle Scene
From *Romulus Buckle & the Engines of War* by Richard Ellis Preston, Jr.

5 — A Sea of Tentacles (Grappling cannon mangled, Martin killed, Buckle grabbed and freed)

6 — A Desperate Charge (Kraken drags Sabrina away, Buckle charges with pistol & axe)

Dispatched on a rescue mission, the Pneumatic Zeppelin's 200-foot launch, the Arabella, races into the skies over the snowbound mountains of Tehachapi. A bloodfreezer blizzard overtakes the Arabella and axe teams are immediately dispatched to the airship's envelope to cut away accumulating ice. A monstrous alien Kraken appears from the maelstrom and latches onto the Arabella's stern, trapping the axe team stationed there. With his crew members and airship being torn apart, Captain Romulus Buckle leads a desperate charge to hold the kraken off until reinforcements arrive.

8 — Last Rescue (Buckle chops Sabrina free of tentacle as Kraken corpse slides off stern)

7 — Killing the Kraken (Buckle kills the beastie)

The DIY Approach

For the artist/maker contingent of the Steampunk/retro-futurist community, DIY is totally natural; there is always work to be done with one's hands. But what does the DIY ethic mean for a storyteller?

Traditionally with storytelling, we think of modes in fiction: novel, short story, memoir, or prose poem. When it comes to simply putting words on the page, DIY is not just a meaningful concept—it's probably the only option. (Although perhaps its ethos still applies: Our storytellers are forging new worlds and alternative histories, refusing to be restricted to real-life events, even if it sometimes means reinventing the wheel.)

However, when we get into more complex, immersive modes of story-telling, DIY becomes a more applicable and relevant concept. And once again, Steampunkers, who in many cases are starting from scratch to tell the stories they are determined to bring to life, are not afraid to take matters into their own hands or approach creative challenges head-on.

"I consider myself a writer most of all," remarks Suna Dasi, "but slowly and surely the making of things has crept upon me over the past two years. In order to create visual accompaniments to the stories, I have had to seriously think through plausible Steampunk costumes for native women, in settings that enhance their identity and function in a Steampunk Indian society. Sewing isn't my forte, but altering, embellishing, and modifying are fast becoming a great source of joy. In our affiliated group, we have a main designer and seamstress and she is very gifted and innovative. We also have a mad female inventrix, and the smells, smoke, and grindings from her workshop are truly something!"

Or consider interactive artist Elizabeth LaPensée, whose painstaking animation process speaks to the care and respect with which she handles the Native American stories that inform her short films and graphic art. "I created characters and landscapes using shells, beads, bone, leather, copper, birch, pinecones, modified and then animated moving assets pixel by pixel in the image-editing software Adobe Photoshop, which were then exported as individual screenshots and compiled using the film-editing software Final Cut Pro."

Projects like LaPensée's suggest a strong connection between art, making, and storytelling. Collaborations can also have the same effect: something made suggesting something told. For example, Jake von Slatt's imaginary machines, created for the anthology *The Thackery T. Lambshead Cabinet of Curiosities*, tell their own story of their creation, but also served as inspiration for writers Annalee Newitz and Charlie Jane Anders to create their own fictions about the machines.

"These were really an enjoyable project for me, and a bit of a departure," von Slatt says. "There's a certain freedom in building something purely for its aesthetics, something that does not have to *work*. Most of the projects I'd done to date were primarily engineering projects done with an artistic eye. These two 'machines' were some of the first one hundred percent art projects and released a part of my creative instinct that had previously been shackled by the need for something to work, and work reasonably well. I think they were so enjoyable to build because they were not Steampunk versions of a thing, as so much Steampunk art is. They were ostensibly artifacts, incompletely understood objects with vague pedigrees. They didn't have to work but needed to look like they could."

ABOVE
Elizabeth LaPensée. Photo by Red Works Photography.

LEFT
The Thackery T. Lambshead Cabinet of Curiosities, edited by Ann and Jeff VanderMeer (HarperCollins, 2006).

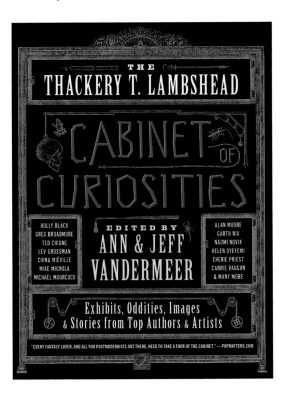

THE
THACKERY T. LAMBSHEAD

CABINET OF CURIOSITIES

HOLLY BLACK
GREG BROADMORE
TED CHIANG
LEV GROSSMAN
CHINA MIÉVILLE
MIKE MIGNOLA
MICHAEL MOORCOCK

EDITED BY
ANN & JEFF
VANDERMEER

ALAN MOORE
GARTH NIX
NAOMI NOVIK
HELEN OYEYEMI
CHERIE PRIEST
CARRIE VAUGHN
& MANY MORE

Exhibits, Oddities, Images
& Stories from Top Authors & Artists

"EVERY FANTASY LOVER, AND ALL YOU POSTMODERNISTS OUT THERE, NEED TO TAKE A TOUR OF THE CABINET." —POPMATTERS.COM

Objects as Narrative: Jake von Slatt's Fake Machines

Von Slatt's description of the parts that went into both pieces is a story unto itself.

What he calls the Chronoclasmic Inhibitor "was the more fantastical of the two pieces. The starting point was the bell jar, found at the swap shop at our town's rubbish transfer station. . . . Once the 'envelope' for the piece was established, I collected a big box of likely parts from my 'warehouse' and sat down to see which fit together the best. The base is from a vintage table lamp, probably about circa 1940. . . . The marble plinth was from the base of another, more modern lamp. In fact, all of the brass parts in the midsection are lamp components."

The two hard drive platters on top of the plinth are made of "aluminum with a thin platinum alloy coating and have a beautiful 'dark mirror' look. The central component of the piece is a cast-glass jewel from the local craft store. Crystals are iconic centerpieces, even in science fiction ('Captain! The dilithium crystals canna take the strain!'). If you want to imbue something with mystical power, put a crystal at the center of it."

The bits of true tech in the piece are even more interesting. "The clockwork at the bottom is from an electromechanical timer. . . . I found it about twenty years ago in a dumpster behind a company that specialized in making instruments for monitoring the environment as well as nuclear weapon tests! The brown-and-blue cloth-insulated wire is not as old as it looks, but is from a specialized application. It is one strand of wire from the inside of an elevator control cable. I found a ten-foot leftover length of the cable in the mud at a building site when I was about fifteen. This is the very last of it; marvelous stuff!

"Finally, the white cotton sheath that looks like shoelace is an actual vintage telephone insulation material. I got to talking to the technician that came out to my house to install my new fiber-optic Internet service; he was a career lineman. After showing him some of my projects, he said, 'I have something for you,' and he gave me a roll that must have a thousand feet of this stuff on it. The stuff was once used for insulating cable splices on telephone poles and underground vaults. The lineman would solder the two strands of wire in a cable that had a hundred-plus strands, and then slip a section of this 'shoelace' over the joint. The connection would be dipped in a pot of hot wax (that must have been fun to carry up the pole!) to seal it from the weather. The whole thing would then be wrapped in more cotton and saturated with wax before being sealed in a lead casing. The little bit of red you see at the top of the piece is where I dipped the lace in some hot wax to acknowledge that heritage.

"Meanwhile, the 'Bassington brain' came together from an odd selection of components, which included a military-spec photodiode that I believe was used in an instrument that measured runway visibility at airports in the sixties and seventies. The other bit of military-spec hardware in this piece is the silver hermetically sealed relay near the bottom of the jar. I almost didn't include it because it was so beautifully made I wanted to put it in a piece of equipment that actually worked!

"The rest of the components all came from a vintage 1940s vacuum-tube tester. I found this tube tester in the trash when I was in grade school and it sat in my parents' attic until they needed the storage a couple of years ago. It's nearly identical to the one I used as a TV technician in my early career. It was beautifully constructed, certainly by hand, with many precision wire-wound resistors and high-quality condensers. It was a piece of test equipment and had to be accurate and stable. The most beautiful parts, I think, are the wiring harnesses, and these I extracted and resoldered to the components in the 'brain' with care to preserve their organic-sense, brainlike folds."

All of these elements suggested a mechanical brain to von Slatt. "It seems natural that a component of this sort would come with a test fixture that would also serve as a tabletop base when it was being worked on by a technician. A vintage portable typewriter case fit the bill, and I adorned it with a few bits of vintage electronic test equipment and test equipment nameplates from the same era as the tube tester."

Storytellers and fiction writers can certainly take inspiration from this process charted by von Slatt. If you look closely—and use your imagination—simple objects can contain entire secret lives, and obsolete technology can point to fascinating pieces of alternate history.

OPPOSITE
Chronoclasmic Inhibitor by Jake von Slatt
ABOVE
Bassington Brain by Jake von Slatt

With von Slatt's artifacts as inspiration, Anders and Newitz created their own narratives:

Mooney & Finch Somnotrope by Charlie Jane Anders. These sleep simulators have become rare artifacts—even though they were mass-produced in the Mooney & Finch Sheffield facility, each one of them emerged as a unique object due to the pressures of the oneiric centrifuge. And they were only sold for three months, prior to the first reports of somnambulism addiction and peripatetic insomnia. The idea of experiencing four or five hours of sleep within a mere few minutes held almost unlimited allure for the world's busiest captains of industry and harried matrons. But few were prepared for the intoxication of the Somnotrope's soothing buzz, the sheer pleasure of watching its central piston raise and lower, gently at first and then with increasing vigor, until one's mind flooded with dream fragments and the impression of having sailed to the nether kingdom and back, all in a few minutes. It only took a few unfortunate deaths for the whole line to be recalled.

Von Slatt Harmonization Device by Annalee Newitz: NAME system and method for cultural transmission scrambling. Patent application number: 15/603976. Assignee: Harmonization Incorporated. Summary of the invention: In the colonies, cultural information is passed from one entity to another using data storage devices accessed psionically via instructional facilities. It is the object of this device to locate, demodulate, and scramble cultural transmissions passing between hostile social formations. This novel device allows operators to inject false vernacular and traditions into cultural signals as they pass between entities. It can also hijack signals carrying historical intelligence by providing a stronger signal on the same frequency. Fig. 1 illustrates an ideal system, where the knobs on the lower right demodulate cultural transmissions, and the amplifier beneath the bell transmits a psionic signal that can reach any analog neurological entity within seven thousand kilometers.

On top of that, von Slatt has his own story for both objects: "The one with the red jewel is a Chronoclasmic Inhibitor and it effects the perception of the passing of time by the human brain—not time itself, mind you, but its perception. The other is a Bassington & Smith Electro-Mechanical Analog Brain, about as smart as a common house cat. It was built to manage the systems aboard an ocean liner and was salvaged from its wreckage. A rather predictable and foolish adventure, really. I mean, whose bright idea was it to put a cat in charge of a vessel that displaced thirty-two thousand tonnes?"

Sometimes, inspiration can be as simple as a strange object, a mysterious artifact, or an enigmatic image.

THE **Bookman Histories**

LAVIE TIDHAR

Steampunk Collections

LEFT

Steampunk III: Steampunk Revolution, edited by Ann VanderMeer (Tachyon, 2012). Cover design by Elizabeth Story.

RÍGHT

Steaming into a Victorian Future, edited by Julie Anne Taddeo and Cynthia J. Miller (Scarecrow Press, 2013). Cover design by Devin Watson.

What you choose to say using Steampunk as your genre is an expression of your unique attributes as a writer—and many choose Steampunk because its popularity allows them to get their ideas across to a larger audience than they might otherwise reach. Steampunk anthologies in translation, such as the recent *Plnou Parou* by Czech editor Martin Šust, are bringing authors like Tobias Buckell, Jeffrey Ford, Jay Lake, and Carrie Vaughn to an enthusiastic readership abroad. In a sense, the bigger Steampunk has gotten commercially, the more it, ironically, allows cutting-edge ideas and philosophies to be expressed within that "broad church." More and more, anthologies like *Steampunk World* (edited by Sarah Hans, and launched and funded via Kickstarter) and *Steampunk Revolution* (edited by Ann VanderMeer) are showcasing the next generation of Steampunk writers: not necessarily based in the United States or the UK.

The anthology *Steamfunk* is another showcase for different perspectives, and another example of the DIY impulse, if in a different direction. It began, according to coeditor Milton Davis, "as a discussion among writers about Steampunk. We were discussing how most Steampunk stories and images don't incorporate the black experience during that time period. Since I've done a few anthologies and I'm a doer rather than a talker, I suggested we do an anthology of stories told from our perspective. When the question of a title came up, Maurice Broaddus, a talented writer who had published a Steampunk story titled 'Pimp My Airship,' said he called what he writes 'Steamfunk.' And there you have it."

What is Steamfunk? "To me, [it] is the incorporation of African and African American culture into the Steampunk movement. It's more than just wearing the Victorian costumes; it's about expressing the situation and culture of people of African descent during the time period on which Steampunk is based. I think Steamfunk, at least as how we interpret it, has been the first to discuss the Victorian era from a black perspective. British Steampunk is notorious for totally ignoring the issues of other cultures during the time period. American Steampunk has been more inclusive, but most of the stories that have tackled the issue have been from a white writer's perspective. With *Steamfunk* you get a no-holds-barred perspective, which in my opinion expands the vision tremendously."

Coeditor Balogun Ojetade says, "Steamfunk is how I express Steampunk. I call myself—and others who express Steampunk through Steamfunk—a 'Steamfunkateer.' Steamfunk poses important questions about the nature and the future of science, society, and commerce, and issues of race, gender, and class. Most readers of Steamfunk stories will simply enjoy the courageous heroes and heroines, the bone-crushing battle scenes, and the wondrous airships, ether weapons, and mechanical monsters. Others, however, will consider the greatest virtue of Steamfunk to be its power as social commentary—which speaks, sometimes subtly and sometimes quite loudly, of the relation of technology to man, of what it means to be truly free, and the ways in which industrialization affects how we relate to one another."

Davis and Ojetade have extended their collaboration further, funding and producing an indie feature-length film titled *Rite of Passage*, which expands on one of Davis's stories in the original collection.

BELOW
An image from Will Hindmarch's *Astonishing! An Original Role-playing Card Game*, available to play as an exclusive original online add-on to this book. This kind of interactive storytelling is one way readers can curate their own stories and narratives. Art by Jeremy Zerfoss.

Illustrating the Steampunk Story: Thoughts from Award-winning Art Director Irene Gallo

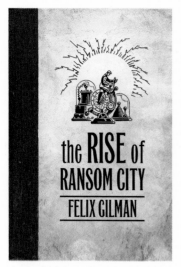

ABOVE
The Rise of Ransom City
by Felix Gilman (Tor, 2012).
Cover art by Ross MacDonald.
OPPOSITE ABOVE
Jon Foster's illustration for
"Lightbringers and Rainmak-
ers" by Felix Gilman (Tor.com,
October 2010).
OPPOSITE BELOW
*The Mad Scientist's Guide to
World Domination*, edited by
John Joseph Adams. Cover
art by Ben Templesmith (Tor,
2013).

The Rise of Ransom City, **Felix Gilman**

Sometimes being simple is the way to stand out.

The Rise of Ransom City is written as an old-fashioned memoir tracing the life of an industrialist building a grand city with the help of a questionable source of light and electricity. I went to let-terpress artist Ross MacDonald to create a cover reminiscent of an earlier era. Ross hand-set the title and author type from his collec-tion of nearly 400 wood and metal fonts. He also created the logo/dingbat representing an idealized vision of the protagonist as an agent of science and industrialization. It's fun to create an actual cover using physical objects, but ultimately, of course, the piece was photographed and digitized for our own mass production.

Since the Steampunk aesthetic can often be defined by its visual complexity and great attention to details, it's easy to imagine *Ransom City* (and its predecessor, *The Half-Made World*) standing out on the shelves next to the usual array of full-color, highly ren-dered artwork on science fiction and fantasy covers, while harking back to the nineteenth century through the very process by which its cover was created. That's the hope, anyway.

"Lightbringers and Rainmakers," Felix Gilman

This was an interesting opportunity. "Lightbringers and Rainmakers" allowed us to dive more deeply into the visual world first explored in a set of novels. "Lightbringers" is a work of short fiction meant to act as back-ground material, or introduction, to Felix Gilman's *The Half-Made World* and *The Rise of Ransom City.* Where we opted for simple icons on the covers of those two novels, here we could zoom in and more fully render an impres-sion of the world these stories inhabit. I asked artist Jon Foster to tackle this project for us since the figures he paints often embody a nineteenth-century sensibility.

As with *Ransom City,* we focused on the light-making apparatus. That, combined with the pose of the character on the right, suggests a kind of progress and technology marching forward—but on closer examination we get a hint of a more nefarious narrative. It would have been tough to get away with such a busy and subtle image on a book cover, but when dealing with a magazine illustration, we can often showcase artwork that rewards more time spent with it.

The Mad Scientist's Guide to World Domination, edited by John Joseph Adams

The fun of anthologies is that you get to work with the overall theme of the book without being beholden to one particular story. Since there is horror and often a little bit of perverse humor characterizing these stories of mad scientists, I thought it was a great opportunity to work with well-known comic book artist Ben Templesmith. His work often focuses on horror, but his stylization and cartooning let his images remain palatable and even fun. It allowed us to use an image that might appear too horrific if it were played straight. That, plus a little bit of over-the-top humor in the copy, is a way to cue the reader that there may be horror here, but it'll be a fun ride as well. Designer Peter Lutjen did the type layout, which, while fairly simple, does an excellent job of setting up hierarchies and presenting a lot of information in a way that draws the reader in and doesn't crowd the art.

EVERYTHING THE FRIENDLY LOCAL EVIL GENIUS NEEDS . . . TO BE INVINCIBLE!

THE MAD SCIENTIST'S GUIDE TO WORLD DOMINATION

EDITED BY **JOHN JOSEPH ADAMS**

ALL ORIGINAL, ALL NEFARIOUS, ALL CONQUERING TALES FROM THE MEGALOMANIACAL PENS OF **DIANA GABALDON, AUSTIN GROSSMAN, SEANAN McGUIRE, NAOMI NOVIK, DANIEL H. WILSON**, AND 17 OTHER EVIL GENIUSES

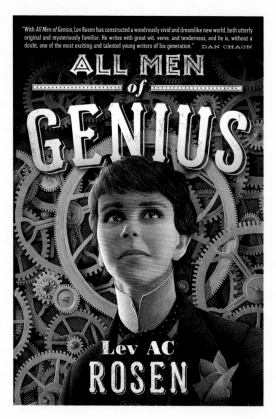

All Men of Genius, Lev Rosen

All Men of Genius, Lev Rosen

All Men of Genius is a *Twelfth Night*–esque tale about a young woman disguising herself as a man to enter a system that allows only males—in this case, a science academy. I'd wanted to work with scratchboard artist Scott McKowen for some time, ever since I first became aware of his work from a series of Broadway posters I saw on the streets of New York. The scratchboard technique is, of course, reminiscent of nineteenth-century engravings.

The trick here was getting the right balance between male and female. The typefaces were also chosen to mimic nineteenth-century newspaper or poster design. And, of course, the gears give the cover an unmistakable Steampunk quality. It is often said that we have about three seconds to stop a reader in their tracks and convince them to pick up a book. After that, the job of selling the book usually falls to the copy, maybe the quotes, or the few pages a potential reader might sample. With so little time to make a first impression, relying on instantly recognizable signifiers can mean the difference between the book being picked up or ignored.

ABOVE
All Men of Genius by Lev AC Rosen (Tor, 2011). Cover art by Scott McKowen.
OPPOSITE ABOVE
Benjamin Carré's illustration for "Zeppelin City" by Eileen Gunn and Michael Swanwick (Tor.com, October 2009).
OPPOSITE BELOW
David Malki's illustration for "The Strange Case of Mr. Salad Monday" by G. D. Falksen (Tor.com, October 2009).

"Zeppelin City," Eileen Gunn and Michael Swanwick

"Zeppelin City" is a strange and action-packed adventure that takes place in a rich urban setting. I wanted something a little steampunk, a little noir, and a bit gritty to boot. An art director friend turned me on to the work of Benjamin Carré and he absolutely fit the bill. (So much of art direction comes down to good casting.) Carré was able to capture the feeling of a claustrophobic city with adventure happening between the cracks. The slight tilt in the composition gives the static elements of the architecture some life. The scale of the buildings and the zeppelins next to the figure in the gyrocopter signal to the reader that there is going to be a lot happening here, and it will be these individuals that'll make the difference. . . .

"The Strange Case of Mr. Salad Monday," G. D. Falksen

"The Strange Case of Mr. Salad Monday" is a playful story that imagines our current conversations and evolution of language, through social media and texting, in a nineteenth-century world. David Malki, perhaps best known for his web comic *Wondermark*, was the perfect artist for this story. His pen-and-ink drawings intentionally mimic newspaper illustrations of the time. The illustration, showing a massive printing press as well as the paper itself, is all about the dissemination of information, now and in the past—and we also get to see gears in action!

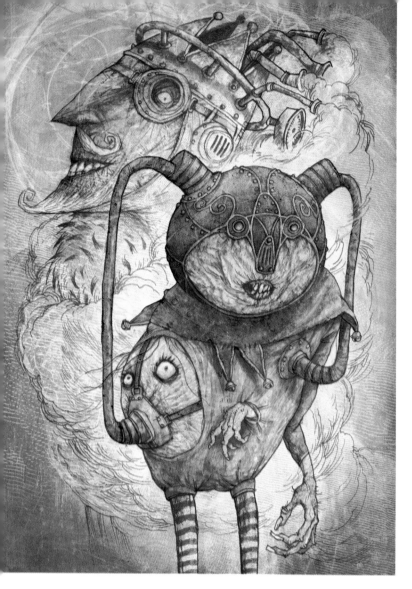

The Working Process

For a storyteller, the working process can be circuitous and convoluted. Sometimes, working doesn't look like working. . . . It can involve reading, scribbling, and lots and lots of daydreaming.

But in terms of elements specifically important to Steampunk storytellers, research ranks right up there. While a vivid imagination and dazzling flights of fantasy are definitely beneficial, solid scientific details and true-to-life historical facts can help ground the story in reality. And grounding the story in reality will make it a lot more engaging and interesting to read.

Lawrence Kasdan, the American producer and screenwriter who contributed to illustrious projects such as *The Empire Strikes Back* and *Return of the Jedi*, once commented, "Being a writer is like having homework every night for the rest of your life." Our Steampunk storytellers are no exception. Here's how a few of them approach the "homework" that informs their creative work.

"With the novel," says Anna Chen, "I'm having to make myself an expert in a wide range of subjects: history, botany, geology, geography, physics, aerodynamics, gender politics . . . but I like the challenge and quite enjoy the idea of being some sort of Renaissance woman if I work hard enough." Overall, Steampunkers tend to be a pretty literate bunch . . . indeed harking back to the days when Renaissance men and women were celebrated in drawing rooms across the continent . . . and Chen's wide-ranging curiosity and lengthy reading list is not an exception, more the norm.

Author Kit Cox comments, "I do a lot of research of historical facts and try and weave as many in around the plot. I like the fact that a lot of history is stranger than any fiction I could write."

Diana Pho agrees. "I would go to the library and spend whole days not writing, but reading sources and jotting notes about where certain things would be useful. I personally love the research part as much as I do the writing!"

ABOVE
Extremes of Retrofuturist Inspiration by Ivica Stevanovic. Original to this volume.

OPPOSITE
Jaclyn Dolamore. Photo by Dade W. Bell.

For some, the research can begin months or years before they start writing—it can take that long for inspiration and atmosphere to percolate into concrete ideas. "Summer of 2009, I was in New York City hunting down books on Weimar Berlin at the Strand, and I started writing my Weimar Berlin–inspired novel in the beginning of 2011," says Jaclyn Dolamore. "So I plan ahead. It's pretty normal for me to have read ten good research books dealing with a time, place, or scenario before I even start."

Jedediah Berry is also a dedicated planner. "I make charts," he tells us. "Or I write things on index cards and shuffle them. Or I outline obsessively, knowing that I'll probably abandon the outline, but trusting that some bright, tiny thing will merge from the mess. Then I write my way toward it." Berry offers us another example of the way that the storyteller's work doesn't always feel productive, even when it is. Cutting four-fifths of an outline doesn't *feel* like an efficient way to work, but sometimes it produces the best final results.

Richard E. Preston explains that, because his background is in screenwriting, he is "partial to scribbling all of my scenes and character beats down on index cards and tacking them up on big bulletin boards. I build this mosaic of cards early on in the process. I like to be able to see the outline of my story, and these cards represent the skeletal structure, which I flesh out as I proceed. This is not a limiting or static process by any means—I rarely write linearly and spend a lot of time adding, removing, and rearranging the cards as the story develops."

Suna Dasi, whose work focuses on placing her characters into a specific cultural context, outlines some of the considerations she keeps in mind as she develops an interesting, well-rounded, and realistic world. "I start by thinking of the things I would like to see, and this can be inspired by any kind of thought. What would a Steampunk temple dancer's day be like? From there I will flesh out the actual story. I will do research and make notes regarding the overarching subject. . . . Very often I will walk into historical aspects that are challenging, and then I have to think about either incorporating them and giving them my own slant or commentary through the story or make a decision to ignore it. For characters that appear in a photo gallery, I choose again what I would like to see, then work out a minor backstory if they appear independent from the narrative. After that, the fun starts: What are they wearing? Do they use weaponry, laboratory equipment? Is their jewelry indicative of their trade or identity?"

Many storytellers find that once the characters come to life, the rest is easy (well, relatively easy). These imaginary people often begin walking, talking, and acting of their own accord, creating the tensions and conflicts that fuel a good story. Of course, once those walking, talking characters get into a few scrapes, the storyteller may find they've plotted themselves into a corner . . . just one of many setbacks that can derail a narrative project before it begins. How does the intrepid storyteller confront such challenges? Read on.

Dealing with Challenges

Even for a very successful creative person, roadblocks can unfortunately come in a lot of forms. Some of them have to do with the nitty-gritty of the creative process itself and others have to do with the inevitable setbacks and frustrations that come with any career—conquering fear of failure and bouncing back from rejection.

"When I was younger, it was very hard to follow through with a whole novel," says Jaclyn Dolamore. "Nowadays, I know that if I'm stuck it's probably because I took a wrong turn somewhere or that a particular scene is just boring and should probably go, but back then if I got stuck I'd be paralyzed and usually drop the whole thing. I didn't know how to rework a story."

Through years of practice, Dolamore has honed her craft and gained confidence; now she knows how to work through those narrative road-blocks and creative cul-de-sacs. However, she admits that sometimes the self-doubt remains. "Those are the days when you start comparing yourself to other writers, or think of the worst reviews you've ever received. That mood can hit me out of nowhere, and hit hard, so one day everything is going beautifully and the next day I'm in the depths of despair. What gets me past it now is experience. I've gone through so many different ups and downs so many times that I can usually talk myself out of them just by reminding myself of a previous time I felt the same."

Though Maurice Broaddus is an experienced writer, he is no stranger to plot problems either, nor to the process of taking a story apart to put it back together again. His Steamfunk short story "Pimp My Airship" was in some ways a tiny window into a vast, vivid imaginary world just waiting to be realized. Urged by colleagues, he decided to turn it into a novel . . . but ran into some challenges along the way. "I thought I was well into it at one point, but then I realized it was broken. So I (literally) dissected the novel. Broke it down into its bits and realized I had three works in there. . . . But now I think I have a sufficient handle on it to finally make a go of it. I'm muscling through chapter three as we speak."

Bottom line: When it comes to dealing with story problems, recalcitrant characters, plot holes, and writer's block, having a bigger bag of tricks goes a long way.

The psychological aspects, however, can be a little trickier. Karin Lowachee, author of *The Gaslight Dogs*, recommends accepting and even embracing challenges as part of the process. "All of those mishaps and frustrations occur so you can make your work better, and that's ultimately what I want. I will do anything to make the work better. In fact, to make the work the best thing I've written up to that moment. That's always the goal. I don't look at writing as a means to just write. I look at it as a means to improve my writing. And in that sense, I welcome the frustrations and process."

Tobias Buckell agrees: "Grit has always been my way through." But it certainly hasn't been easy; he's conquered a lot of challenges along the way.

"I was never the kid everyone pointed to and said, 'That guy is going to be a full-time writer.' I had dyslexia, ADHD, and horrible spelling issues. I got bad grades. I mean, yeah, I read a lot, but I had a lot of work to do. I started out fumbling, and I've just been trying to iterate something slightly better over and over again (and often not succeeding). Every artist has their own methods, but I try to finish even an uneven project, because for me a crappy existing draft is better than the most perfect nonexistent thing I'll ever write."

So when the going really gets tough, what to do? Kit Cox has a somewhat offbeat suggestion: Legos. "Any problem can be made better with Legos," he says. "If you can't make stuff with Legos, then Google Image 'Steampunk Lego' and just smile."

If Legos don't work for you, however, try Suna Dasi's approach: "A lot of tea and swearing. But always going back and trying again."

Seven Pieces of Advice for
New Writers

1. "***Seek* originality.** It's your duty to innovate, to be different, to tell a new story in a new way. And don't tell me originality is dead. You're just being too lazy or too scared of failing life."

—Jacques Barcia

2. "Every writer works differently. But often I think that the big idea must be put aside in favor of the word, the sentence, the paragraph. **Let the LANGUAGE and the CRAFT lead you to the idea:** Where you end up will likely be something more vital than the notion with which you began. I think of writing as a means of exploration; it's worthwhile because you don't know exactly what's out there." —*Jedediah Berry*

3. "My own practical experience was to keep it focused, at least to begin with. *The Bookman* is one hero, one point of view. Having just the one character helped me keep it more grounded, to see the world through one set of eyes, to explore it gradually. By *The Great Game*, I allowed myself three different braiding stories, but by then I had a better idea—I hope!—of what I was doing. **Always look for the personal story.** World-building is cool but it doesn't make a novel, it makes a manual. And have fun! I think that's the most important thing you can do." —*Lavie Tidhar*

4. "**Whatever your process, just do it at some point. DON'T GIVE UP if you have a passion for that idea.** Don't be intimidated by big ideas. This is why knowing yourself as a person and as a writer is so important. You won't know otherwise when the 'right time' is. I have grand ideas, but I know I'm not a good enough writer to tackle them yet. And that's perfectly all right. I'll work on other things until I'm at that point." —*Karin Lowachee*

5. "**Don't be afraid** of 'not being original.' Because, c'mon, this is Steampunk first of all, which is so derivative and full of tropes that you should not be afraid to engage them in your work at first. Just don't be afraid to break away from these tropes, either." —*Diana Pho*

6. "I'm a big fan of *forcing* **yourself** to START creating, and just **working** and **working** till you have something in front of you—and, yeah, that something is probably awful, but now you can rework it, reshape it, make it into something good, and you don't have all that pressure to start anymore. That's a lot of pressure. If someone is stuck on just a big picture or concept and doesn't have an idea for characters or plot, then I'd say try to find a small moment or image, symbolic of the big idea, and start there. Just write it. Then keep writing. Or, if that doesn't work, just steal something from Shakespeare." —*Lev Rosen*

7. "Sometimes, you JUST have to *get out of your own way*. In a certain chapter in *Here, There Be Dragons*, I needed a talking animal to drive a steam-powered car—an animal I hadn't really planned out. I picked a badger, because talking badgers are cool—and he was so much fun to write. By the time I got to the third book in the series, not only was he still around, but one scene had twenty talking badgers on a fire engine. Who knew?" —*James A. Owen*

Writing Exercises: Repurposing Art

by Matthew Cheney

Images are essential to great fiction, and fiction for centuries has been accompanied by images, sometimes definitively (what would Sherlock Holmes be without Sidney Paget's pictures?). When images are approached creatively, with the writer seeking out the details, the missing links, and the odd associations, they can be potent sources of inspiration. The idea is not to illustrate the illustration but to let it fuel and spark imagination.

To that purpose, we've provided the painting on pages 178–179 and a collection of writing exercises. The painting depicts a rather retro-futurist scene, but the exercises do not require a specific genre, because the imaginative work necessary for this sort of inspiration is common to most fiction writing. Let your visions wander where they will.

Some exercises will lead you to create raw material (the writerly equivalent of doodles and sketches), while others may lift you toward an entire poem, story, novel, or novel sequence. Some of the exercises may help with particular skills (characterization, worldbuilding), while others simply promote healthy imaginative habits. They're not presented in any particular order; rather, they are a toolbox, a paintbox, a toybox—a cabinet of curiosities waiting for you to try something unexpected.

- Write a newspaper report about this international aviation event.
- Who is riding in the blimp? Where do they come from, and what did they expect to see today? Are they enjoying their ride so far?
- A famed poet sailed in one of the balloons that day, and the rest of the poet's career was devoted to commemorating all that happened. Transcribe the poet's poems, or provide brief excerpts in a critical study.
- Describe the landscape below the image.
- Several highly literate birds were present that day, though they are not visible in the picture. Some of them went on to sell their stories to the tabloid press. Write one of those stories.
- In the next thirty-seven seconds, three things will happen at once in this scene. What are they?
- After the event depicted in this image, more postcards were mailed than at any other time in many years. Write a selection of the most interesting postcards sent that day . . . and at least one of the least interesting.
- Who is the shark escaping from? Explain.
- The shark was known for speaking in fragments and riddles. This, it was later discovered, had an important scientific purpose. What was it, and why was it so important on the day the shark flew among the balloons and dirigibles?
- One of the world's greatest opticians studied the event depicted here and made extraordinary advances in the science of lenses and vision afterward. Why? Tell the story.

OVERLEAF

The Mad King and His Odd Airships, original artwork by Ivica Stevanovic. Original to this volume.

- Art historians long considered this painting (rumored to be the work of Wallace Tillinghast) to have been lost. Little was known about it until it was recently discovered in the basement of a library in Budapest. How did it get to that library, and why was it never discovered before now? How does it change our understanding of the work of Tillinghast? Why did so many newspapers refuse to report the discovery? Where is the painting now?
- The colors in this painting are mostly not accurate to the event, or so some art critics argue. The painter left a confession in which the coloring was explained, and this caused some critics and viewers much anger. Write that confession.
- This painting was made after the painter's father related a story he had been told by an itinerant accountant in a remote tavern quite a few years before. Write that story.
- This image is most famous for being in a popular advertisement. Write the text for that advertisement.
- The man in the foreground of this picture was not at all responsible for what happened to him. Indeed, his story is one of the most amazing tales of being in the wrong place at the wrong time that has ever been told. Tell that story.
- Beards are considered highly subversive personal statements in this world. Why is that, and why is the man in the foreground bearded?
- The man in the foreground of the picture was well known for having failed at every business venture he attempted before the one great success that brought him here. The nature of that success, though, is in dispute. Write an interview with two Wikipedia editors who keep rewriting the man's Wikipedia entry.
- For many years, this painting hung upside-down in a museum. No one complained. Why not? What caused the museum finally to turn the painting around?
- Every object you see in this picture is, to some extent at least, conscious and sentient. Transcribe the thoughts of the item that you are most surprised to discover has thoughts.
- A team of aviation engineers gathered to study this image. Their conversation went awry, and led to at least one demand for a duel. Write the conversation.
- Certain people have claimed that this image illustrates a scene from a lost play by William Shakespeare. Tell the story of how the play came to be written, how it came to be lost, and how some particularly obsessive scholars have tried to locate and authenticate it.
- A little-known children's book attempted to tell the story of this image through the eyes of a hedgehog. Write a chapter from that book.
- List seven important objects that are not included in this picture. Write a short story in which all of those objects play a pivotal role in how events turn out.
- Write an essay in which you explain how this image is subtly alluded to by five works of literature that no one else has yet realized refer to it.
- If this image were included in an elementary textbook on biology, what chapter would it be in? What page? Write that page.
- A mysterious stranger once walked into a small art gallery, looked at this picture, and then promptly began screaming in a language no one has yet been able to identify. Tell the story of this stranger.
- Several popular works of historical fiction have used the scene depicted here as a climax to their plots, though each work has been vastly different in tone and purpose from the others. Write short passages from each of those historical fictions.
- While the events depicted here were deeply important to many things that would come later, something was happening seventeen miles away that may have been even more consequential, though it didn't seem so at the time. Tell that story.

. . . .

Matthew Cheney's work has been published by *English Journal, One Story, Web Conjunctions, Strange Horizons, Failbetter.com, Ideomancer, Pindeldyboz, Rain Taxi, Locus, The Internet Review of Science Fiction, and SF Site,* among others, and he is the former series editor for *Best American Fantasy.* He has taught Writing at Plymouth State University and the University of New Hampshire State.

THE ENCYCLOPEDIA OF FANTASTIC VICTORIANA: ALTERNATIVE HISTORY EDITION.

DETROIT INSTALLATION. Art installation, as a relatively recent addition to the forms in which art is made, remains, if not controversial, then at least relatively less respected than other art forms.

Art installations have traditionally been an attempt to overcome art's limitations: its commodification—no such commodification of an installation can be created, because once an installation is disassembled and dispersed it is completely gone; art's privileging of the role of museums and galleries—installations often take place outside of them, and further become part of the whole space, a subject, rather than an object within that space; art's privileging of remote viewing, since installations reject the traditional concentration on one object in favor of a consideration of the relationship between a number of competing or complementary elements; and the Wordsworthian "emotion recollected in tranquility," as installations are designed to force the viewer to engage in a heightened, immediate bodily experience of the work. Traditional art objects are passive; art installations are active.

A case in point is the "Detroit Installation," a.k.a. "The Naked Launch." Created by Emily Wagner, with assistance by Jake von Slatt, and loosely based on William S. Burroughs's *The Naked Lunch*, the Detroit Installation took place in Detroit, Michigan, over Memorial Day weekend, 2013. Occupying nine square blocks of the suburb of Chaldean Town, the Detroit Installation was a devastating indictment of American foreign policy in artistic form.

Similar to Tyree Guyton's "Heidelberg Project," the Detroit Installation consisted of a three-by-three square block area, transformed into an unidentified foreign urban location. Carefully-placed rubble and the shells of burned-out cars crowd the streets, and those buildings in the Installation area which were not already rubble or abandoned hulks have been re-shaped to create a more generally Middle- and Near-Eastern urban landscape.

Viewers are given the choice of entering a building, located blocks away in downtown Detroit, or entering the Installation streets. Those entering the building are given name-tags reading "Annexian/Mugwump/Subject." They are also given control of dirigible drones, altered into a "steampunk" appearance by von Slatt, and steam-powered robotic "Liquefactionists," and allowed to strafe the streets, and the other viewers, at will with paint balls of varying sizes.

Those entering the streets are given "Freeland/Object" name-tags and Victorian vests, top hats, goggles, and Empire coats and are let loose in the installation. Viewers are forced to traverse the littered, pseudo-Iranian or pseudo-Afghani streets while enduring a barrage of red paint balls from the Annexian/Mugwump/Subjects. The impact of these paintballs does no permanent damage but assuredly stings. The viewer can pass through or by the "wedding," the "marketplace," and the "University" before reaching the "end" of the installation, Dr. Benway's "White" "House."

Most art critics judge installations on five

planks: **site-specificity**, **temporality**, **cerebrality**, **interactivity**, and **internal process**. The Detroit Installation is profoundly successful on four of these.

The Detroit Installation's site-specificity is superb. The Installation uses the body of the audience—traditionally meaning the interactive immersion of the viewer, but in the Installation a quite literal experience—and the body of the physically ruined suburb of Chaldean Town to incisive effect. The Installation has no discernible physical narrative, apart from the geometric floor plan. There is no focal point within the Installation, and the wedding, marketplace, and university are all unassertive. The confusion between the space of "reality" (Detroit) and the space of subjective construction ("Interzone") works to activate and de-center the viewer, creating a *verfremdungeffekt* from the viewing experience itself.

All installations are temporally limited in ways that "permanent" art (paintings, statues, even palimpsests) is not—but as Freud wrote, "a flower that blossoms for a single night does not to us seem any less lovely." The temporality of the Installation extends along a different vector than many other art installations. Wagner's use of von Slatt's steampunk devices, from the dirigible drones to the robotic paintball guns of the Liquefactionists to the paint-spraying IEDs on the streets, extends her critique across empires and centuries, condemning modern American foreign policy *and* Victorian Britain's empire-making.

Cerebrality emphasizes the concept of the installation over its *impressionismus*, the arousing of emotions in the minds of the viewer—as Marcel Duchamp emphasized with his urinal, the idea is the important element of the art, not the ephemeral emotions aroused or the material object of the art. While some critics define aesthetic enjoyment as the combination of cerebrality and the emotions aroused in the viewer's mind, the Detroit Installation places the emphasis on the *idea* of the Installation, rather than on emotions. The emotions viewers experience, as Mugwump/Subjects or Freeland/Objects, are entirely negative, while the idea of the Installation—its critique—brings forth more positive ideas and inspirations.

On interactivity the Detroit Installation strikes an uneven balance. Those viewers who take the Mugwump/Subject route control the Installation and to an extent the Freeland/Object viewers via the dirigible drones and the Liquefactionists. Those viewers who choose to become Freeland/Objects are *objects*, to be acted upon, although some of von Slatt's creations in the Interzone—the clockwork Mosque, the brass Clock, the geared Guitar, the platformed Bus—allow for limited Object volitionality. Implicitly Wagner forces viewers to take a choice between being actors and being acted-upon, and while this emphasizes her point about drone strikes and US foreign policy it also creates an emotional frustration for many viewers—which does, however, further enhance the *verfremdungeffekt* and force those viewers to question both themselves and their political behavior.

The internal process—the physical matter of the installation itself, and how it functions—is superb. Wagner and von Slatt use a combination of elements to assault the viewer's taste, smell, touch and hearing. Besides the inevitable clouds of coal smoke and the constant sound of gears turning, von Slatt also modified pipe organs to create 18 Hz. infrasound, the frequency at which sound causes humans to feel uneasy and experience mild headaches and even hallucinations—thus adding to the hallucinatory effect of Burroughs's work combined with Wagner and von Slatt's reality.

JESS NEVINS

CHAPTER
4

STEAMPUNK
MUSIC AND
PERFORMANCE

Steampunk music is a force unto itself: a broad, diffuse category, frequently encompassing many other forms of creative expression. Many musicians and performers deliver totally immersive experiences to their audiences, incorporating visual art, elaborate prop making, intricate costume design, and vivid storytelling.

At its core, Steampunk music often creates a soundtrack to an imagined world. All music is deeply personal, but this music is perhaps even more so, in that it adds an extra layer: its maker's vision of an alternate history or an unlikely future.

Because Steampunk musicians are a varied and eccentric bunch, each group approaches this task of musical translation in a different way. In the words of musician and performer Professor Elemental, "Many bands like to build their own little Steampunk universes to live in." The end result is a complex, wonderful profusion of sounds, styles, and songs; for a relatively unknown subgenre, Steampunk music can be a surprisingly wide tent—or, as two of our interviewees both chose to term it, a "broad church." That said, there are two major groups that have emerged within the genre as a whole.

The first group consists of self-proclaimed Steampunk bands: musical acts that have consciously fashioned themselves in the Steampunk image. They frequently play at Steampunk conventions and participate as both artists and fans in the community scene. They create elaborate personas and backstories set in wildly adventurous Victorian-era milieus. They wear fabulous costumes and their performances are often inspired by musical theater: a combination of storytelling and music rolled into one. Take, for example, Abney Park, one of the longest-running acts in the Steampunk music world; the hardworking Voltaire; Professor Elemental ("the mad Steampunk professor"); and the Mechanisms ("Steampunk space pirates").

Some bands, like the Unextraordinary Gentlemen, enjoy the storytelling aspect of their Steampunk universes nearly as much as they enjoy the music making. The Unextraordinary Gentlemen have even supplemented their website with an extensive "Unextraordinary Encyclopedia" that includes a detailed list of people, places, and things related to their imaginary world; it begins with an introduction that includes these slightly ominous remarks:

The following is a record of written material recovered from an abandoned chapel in upstate Connecticut, in these United States. The

ABOVE
Unextraordinary Gentlemen.
Photo by Sid Penance.
LEFT
Stars Pulled Down, 2012
release from the Unextraordi-
nary Gentlemen. Cover art by
Richard Pilawski.

bound manuscript was badly damaged by water, fungus and the ravages of time. It has been estimated to have been written just after the turn of the 20th Century. The contents are more than a passing interest to me for several reasons, not the least of which is this:

Recently, a musical group calling themselves Unextraordinary Gentlemen have emerged from the Los Angeles, California Art-wave scene. The lyrics to their songs contain references to characters, places and events that correspond, almost identically, with the material found in the pages of the rotting book from Connecticut.

Band member Malcom says, "That backstory stuff is pretty much my baby. I have tons and tons of little scraps of characters and plots and places and smells and tastes, et cetera. I throw out hints and shades of this/these universe(s) with the lyrics and the encyclopedia."

Bad September delves into the riches of alternate history to inspire their lyrics. "First we figure out the history, find a compelling personality, and pick a really interesting 'What if?' Then we hypothesize. What if Tesla and Edison had a duel? What if Archduke Franz Ferdinand wasn't shot? How would a steam-powered zeppelin operate? What would the anthem of a communist Britain sound like? Or a Steampunk carnival in Cádiz? We meld real history with Steampunk to create a compelling alternate world, and then build the songs from that. This means we often have lyrics that are rich with meaning, metaphor, and allusions."

The second group of Steampunk songsters is more diffuse, and more difficult to define, as "Steampunk" may be only one of the labels they go by. These bands are also typically quite ambitious and innovative; they set out to accomplish something musically unusual and create an unfamiliar fusion of sounds. Their fans, rather than the bands themselves, are typically the ones who reach for descriptors, perhaps a language to use as they evangelize the music. Other fans — not to mention the bands — may look to equally valid labels.

For the Steampunk-associated performers featured in this chapter, these descriptors include "Victorian grindcore" (The Men That Will Not Be Blamed for Nothing), "carnivalesque world folk" (Crystal Bright), "Dickensian Kate Bush" (Sunday Driver), "mystic country" (The Cassettes), and "Victoriandustrial, glam rock, psychotic vaudeville burlesque" (Emilie Autumn). These categories hold plenty of ambiguity and overlap.

Interestingly, this fusion often exists within a single album or oeuvre. For Max of the Absinthe Drinkers, it's one of the genre's appeals. According to him, "The most liberating part of Steampunk or retro-futurism is how many genres it makes available to you as an artist. Modern pop is so segmented and often really limiting. You know, Lamb of God can't sound like Lady Gaga or both artists' fans would have a stroke. When you get involved in setting poetry to music, suddenly you are allowing the words to point you in a particular direction: Some poems want to be tangos and some poems want to be space-age bachelor pads. This forces you to keep flexible and keep listening to ever-wider sources of inspiration."

Exploration and Adventure: Steampunk's Central Story

So if Steampunk music covers such a varied range of musical styles, what — if anything — is the uniting theme that ties the genre together? In search of a more universal set of descriptors, we turned to our interviewees to ask what they think defines Steampunk music as a genre.

Professor Elemental offers a concise answer: "Politeness, camaraderie, invention . . . exploration and adventure." Richard of the Unextraordinary Gentlemen adds: "The actual sound of Steampunk is all over the map, so in that regard I would leave it up to the individual's music taste. I would hope they would dress the part and that the lyrics conjured up some nice, fantastic imagery. I would definitely have a violin, cello, banjo, accordion, or some instrument that would give it an 'old-timey' feel. And for extra credit, I would add a bit of machinery to the mix by way of electronic instruments or percussive metal elements to represent the fantastic machines, crazy inventions, or the Industrial Revolution in general."

Most agree that Steampunk music remains relatively difficult to define. "There was/is no unifying style associated with the subculture — Steampunk is a massively broad church encompassing everything from neoclassical, old-time folk, and jazz to whimsical hip-hop, world music, electro-swing,

and goth," says Andy of the Men That Will Not Be Blamed for Nothing. This flexibility created an important opportunity for the burgeoning band, as they found an interesting and unexplored niche to fill. Despite the wide variety of musical styles currently embraced by Steampunk, "there was nothing dirty and loud. We decided to take the 'punk' part of Steampunk literally and imagine what a punk band would be singing about if they were from 1880 instead of 1980."

The Lisps are a Brooklyn-based band whose rollicking and lyrically complex music was first labeled as Steampunk not by its creators, but by its fans. The Lisps' singer/songwriter, César Alvarez, says, "In 2008, I started trying to tell a story about a Civil War soldier who was super into proto–science fiction, and then people started telling me it was Steampunk. At that point I had never heard of Steampunk. I've always been interested in music that compressed multiple time periods, so when I came up with the idea it felt native to what I was working on already. I wanted to create music that had the effect of looking at an old artifact at a museum, and then seeing yourself reflected back in the glass of the display case." This story became *Futurity*, a Civil War–era Steampunk musical that has been performed to broad acclaim in Boston and New York.

In fact, Alvarez comments, "We've actually never called ourselves Steampunk. We've never used the term in reference to ourselves that I know of." And while Steampunk fans definitely connected with those elements in *Futurity*, it was also a powerful piece of storytelling with relevance to a much broader audience. As Alvarez describes it, "It is a story about America, and imagination, and our relationship to technology."

Emilie Autumn is another one of those "outsider" musicians who have been embraced by Steampunk fans. (She is also revered by the Gothic Lolita scene. In fact, she has developed her own passionate and totally unique following—a group of dedicated superfans who term themselves the "Plague Rats.")

One thing that does seem to define Steampunk is an embrace of idiosyncrasy, and a disregard for pedestrian practicalities. Emilie Autumn says, "I'm never against fame or popularity, but I have no desire to be mainstream or practical, and I would think the same goes for the Steampunk scene. I mean, there is nothing practical about wearing a cage crinoline, a corset, or oversized golden goggles when your eyesight is perfectly fine. . . . Being impractical is, to me, one of Steampunk's defining characteristics. If it's powered by the tools of the past, it is very likely not going to be the most efficient car/gun/wheelchair/computer/communication device. But practical isn't very romantic, is it?"

On this last point, at least, Chris of the Absinthe Drinkers can agree. He says, "The last thing I would want is for Steampunk to be useful or practical. It's the impracticality that is part of the allure. Practical is boring and repetitive. A corset isn't very practical, but Lord, it is a good look. Just look at the Steampunk mods of consumer electronics: beautiful but impractical. And that, I think, is one of the core concepts of retro-futurism: the beautiful machine."

OPPOSITE
On the set of Professor Elemental's *I'm British* video shoot. Photo by Ben Broomfield.
ABOVE
Sammy Tunis portraying Ada Lovelace in the Lisps' Steampunk musical *Futurity*. Photo by Evgenia Eliseeva, courtesy of American Repertory Theater.
LEFT
Futurity cast. Photo by Evgenia Eliseeva, courtesy of American Repertory Theater.

Anna Chen's
The Steampunk Opium Wars

Anna Chen is a writer, performer, poet, and blogger; her multimedia, genre-crossing works, which often tackle issues of culture, history, and identity, have connected powerfully with both critics and audiences. Commissioned by the National Maritime Museum to create a commemorative event to mark the opening of a new Traders gallery, Chen turned to history—and Steampunk. The Traders gallery—which Chen had also been tapped to co-curate for the season—was designed to preserve the history of the East India Company from the 1600s on. Thus, Chen's production *The Steampunk Opium Wars* was born.

The Opium Wars, which took place in the mid-nineteenth century, were the violent outcome of a bitter trade dispute between imperialist Britain and Qing Dynasty China. Britain's endless thirst for tea (over six million pounds imported a year), and other goods such as silks and spices, had begun to create a severe trade deficit, particularly because China preferred to be paid solely in silver. To redress the balance, British traders began illegally importing opium, cheaply produced in India. Eventually, they were smuggling more than thirty thousand chests a year into China.

"The profits from the opium trade made fortunes, earned revenues for the British government, paid for the administration of the Empire in India and even financed a large slice of Royal Navy costs," says Chen's write-up of the show on her website. "When the Chinese tried to halt the import of the drug, the narco-capitalists persuaded Foreign Secretary Palmerston and Lord Melbourne's government to go to war in 1839. The first military conflict, lasting a bloody three years, resulted in the Treaty of Nanking and the transfer of territory including Hong Kong to British rule." More than twenty thousand Chinese people were killed in the conflict.

It's a sobering tale, and a dark chapter in Britain's history. But as a poet and performer, Chen is experienced in translating sensitive material for her audience. (Her advice to writers: "Read novels for empathy. Observe how emotions work, what drives people, what undercurrents are flowing beneath the surface.") When it came to the heavy material of the Opium Wars, she says, "Rather than tell the story flatly, I wanted to exercise my inventiveness and stimulate the audience's imagination. So, with a combination of poetry, songs, and set pieces from the history, accompanied by some heavy electrified guitar and bass, we brought the story into the belly of the beast and performed it at the Royal National Maritime Museum in February 2012."

The story featured fictional characters, loosely based on real-life figures; the show's war-mongering Sir Jardine Matheson is based on William Jardine and James Matheson, who pushed for war, and its Mr. Cobstone is an amalgam of Richard Cobden and William Gladstone, two activists who opposed it. Prime Minister Lord Palmerston and a laudanum-stoned version of Queen Victoria also appear.

"The night kicked off with the cast selling silver foil wraps of opium (squished malt loaf) to the audience as they came in," says Chen. "Then I entered to a Jimi Hendrixed–up British national anthem played on screeching guitar, like Hendrix's 'Star Spangled Banner.' It was all very jolly. The most moving moments were Captain Ironside recalling the attacks on the Chinese in their own land in order to make them take the East India Company's opium at the point of a gun, and the burning of the beautiful Summer Palace.

"As a sideshow in a room off the main drag, Gary Lammin demonstrated the Hackney Tea Ceremony—like the Chinese tea ceremony, only carried out by a Cockney geezer making mugs of what we call 'builders' tea' (strong PG Tips with too much sugar and slopped up with milk). It was our little joke on orientalism and still makes me laugh."

The Steampunk Opium Wars was performed to nearly three hundred people that evening (something of a record for the museum) and live-streamed to many more. But, Chen says, "the most pleasurable aspect at the end of the night was the number of people who were shocked, surprised, and delighted by the entertainment, and who told us they'd known nothing about the subject."

Inspired by her work on the project, Chen is now working on expanding the story of *The Steampunk Opium Wars* into a novel, titled *The Camellia and the Poppy*. "My imagination has been set loose," she says. "It's an epic sweep, my alternative history of the engagement between two great cultures. There may very well be airships. No goggles yet, but I'm working on it.

"[Steampunk has] turned my world from monochrome to rich sepia tones," says Chen. "Sometimes the limits of a form can be liberating as it gives you a structure. And yet the Steampunk form is still developing. Maybe we're in a glorious golden heyday before it settles into anything rigid—which I fervently hope it never does."

The Dolls of New Albion

A Steampunk Opera

ABOVE
Lauren Osborn as Annabelle in *The Dolls of New Albion*, written by Paul Shapera and directed by Mark Swetz. Photo by Nadia Adame.

BELOW
The Dolls of New Albion album cover art by Marjolijn de Korte.

OPPOSITE
An image from Galway Theatre's production of *Dradin, In Love*, based on the novella of the same name in the book *City of Saints & Madmen* by Jeff VanderMeer. The set design repurposed actual pages from the book, printed with illustrations by Eric Schaller and John Coulthart.

Bringing Steampunk to the Stage

Thanks to an enthusiastic tendency toward storytelling and world-building, many Steampunk music shows have a definite performative aspect. They've already staked out plenty of territory for themselves on the Steampunk stage. But Steampunk, with all its theatricality and drama, offers a real world of performance possibilities.

Finnish band Pepe Deluxé—an envelope-pushing electronic group that bills themselves as an "intercontinental collective orchestra"—offers one example. The band's latest album, *Queen of the Wave*, is "an esoteric pop opera" that draws on the mythology of the lost city of Atlantis, told in the rollicking fashion of an old-style Edisonade, and set to music with an eerily nostalgic flair (samples that sound like they floated in from a long-lost era, instrumentation that includes a Tesla coil synthesizer and a pneumatic percussion machine). The album's deluxe liner notes take the form of a hardcover book filled with stories of historical oddities, retro-style imagery, and nineteenth-century esoterica; snippets of poetry, images of the band, retrofuturistic line art, and kaleidoscopic collage. As band member James Spectrum says, "Almost every page contains something more or less unique, yet more or less true (or claiming to be true). . . . We have already created something that is mixing reality and imagination in a very, very complex way." The result is a truly multimedia, multisensory experience, bringing together a diverse selection of art forms.

Another Steampunk performance still under development is *The Dolls of New Albion*, a Steampunk opera by Paul Shapera. This ninety-minute

ABOVE AND OPPOSITE
Stills from Galway Theatre's
production of *Dradin, In
Love,* based on the novella by
Jeff VanderMeer.

musical portrays a multigenerational saga set in a fantastical city. According to Shapera, "The story begins with lonely scientist Annabelle McAlistair's attempt to bring back her dead love into the body of a mechanical mannequin." As a musician, Shapera worked hard to develop a uniquely "Steampunk" sound for the music, which represents the very heart of the show; for the curious, the soundtrack can be streamed or purchased online. As far as we know, it's the first Steampunk opera in the world. Shapera ultimately plans to develop the musical into a trilogy, and we hear a Dieselpunk opera is also in the works.

A recent production of coauthor Jeff Vander-Meer's "Dradin, In Love" points to some of the challenges of staging science fiction and fantasy. "Dradin" isn't specifically Steampunk, but it does subvert Victorian-era tropes. It's a close weird cousin, like perhaps . . . Squidpunk? The story features a deranged missionary who falls in love with a woman he's never met, only seen in an upstairs window; a Festival of the Freshwater Squid; odd living saints; and several grotesque adventures in an imaginary city called Ambergris that is like a combination of Paris, London, and a metropolis from a more southern clime. Produced by Irish theatre group Tribe in partnership with The Granary Theatre, Cork, the show was also later staged at Galway Theatre Festival. Creator and performer Bob Kelly from the Tribe Theatre group spoke to us about the challenges in bringing the story to stage.

"The stage generally isn't kind to alternate realities," he says. "Reimagined technologies, nonhuman species, 'magic,' speculative fiction—these rarely succeed in theater. The best explanation I've come across for this comes from J. R. R. Tolkien, when he slammed the *Macbeth* witches as daft—he believed that by agreeing to suspend their awareness of the theater and the actors, the audience were already engaged in one false world—and that to ask them to believe in witches and magic was then a step too far. He reckoned that Shakespeare had taken the material for a good novel and made a silly play out of it. So we had to be very careful; the line between fantasy and farce is very thin onstage."

How did Kelly and his troupe get around this problem—and create the right type of world-building on the stage?

"We kept the projections small and distant; the images themselves were neither photos nor video, but simple animated collage pieces—crackly and grainy, very lo-fi. We added the sound of an old slide projector clacking into life. The effect we were aiming for was that of cutting-edge alternate technology—we wanted to conjure up the idea that somewhere backstage there were some little guys frantically pedaling a penny-farthing to get the thing to work. If the show comes around again, I'll work to heighten this—I'd much rather, for example, project onto a filthy glass lens than onto a rectangular screen."

The basic aim was to give everything in the play the right edge of weirdness, "familiar yet strange," to convey the story's "gothic tone, urban setting, the looming architecture, the variety and danger on every street, the selling of corpses to willing buyers; the sense of a massive and barely repressed rabble, prone to violent rioting or celebrating; a certain sense of opulence or decadence in the richness of the imagery and language.

"As a reference, we worked in part with the art nouveau style from the turn of the century—in particular its architecture and furniture, the curves, parabolas, and plantlike forms, which were reminiscent of the squid references that permeated the story."

This approach worked well to dramatize a text that "works subtly and skillfully to stop the reader from thinking that they understand the world's boundaries. Early in the story, for example, automobiles are mentioned, but only briefly; the inclusion of technologies such as this—while not defining or explaining how they fit within the world—plays against our preconceptions of the world that have been conjured up by the 'Victorian' imagery; in this way, the piece keeps us open to anything being possible."

Another great example of Steampunk staging is a recent production of Karin Tidbeck's short story "Beatrice," also featured in this chapter. Instead of human actors, this innovative production by Swedish drama troupe Tidsrum relies on the expressive capabilities of hand-crafted puppets. Conveying fantastic elements with both subtlety and flair can be a challenging undertaking, but fortunately, it can be done. And when it's done well, the results are magical in the best way.

"Building a Utopian Playland": Steampunk and Performance

by Diana M. Pho

ABOVE
Diana Pho. Photo by Rachael Shane.

OPPOSITE
The League of S.T.E.A.M. Photo credit: Los Productions LLC.

What qualifies as Steampunk making? At first, that seems like an easy question to answer. A modded computer. A well-cut, nineteenth-century-inspired dress. An intricate gear-work necklace. A prop gun that shoots out Nerf darts or roars like a fire engine when the trigger is pulled. When it comes to theater and performance, however, can you "make" a Steampunk *experience*?

The theatricality inherent in Steampunk objects is undeniable. They become characters themselves and have to explain two backstories: the technical one—"How did you make it?"—and the fantastical one, which is usually a highly embellished version of how the Steampunk character (cutely referred to as a "steamsona") built this, and perhaps, a detailed explanation of how this invention uses electric eels, etheric energy, or sonic waves to function. The Steampunk aesthetic brings a heightened sense of imagination to its craftwork, because the art is also expected to act larger than life and tell its own story.

Mainstream interpretations of Steampunk performances aren't hard to miss. There are highly stylized music videos of Panic! at the Disco, Justin Bieber, Lady Gaga, and Rush. Syfy's *Warehouse 13* sported gadgets invented by H. G. Wells and Nikola Tesla. NBC's *Dracula* arguably became the "Steampunk TV show" currently on-air as soon as people noticed the gears turning in the opening credits. Often, however, the lot of Steampunk performers isn't as appreciated by those outside the community, even though missing their presence is like not seeing the forest for the trees.

Steampunk performance manifests itself in a variety of ways. Firstly, the vintage arts—which have their roots in the nineteenth century—are being given renewed life: burlesque, pinups, vaudeville, circus acts, belly dancing. Enrique Velazquez, otherwise known as Doc Quincy E. Quartermain (Doctor Q for short), is a Steampunk DJ who also runs the Artifice Club out of Atlanta, Georgia. The Artifice Club is an organization dedicated to fostering the vintage arts. He views the performers he supports and the events he creates as intricately tied to Steampunk's innate creativity: "What Steampunk brings to the table is the spirit of reappropriation that the maker movement pioneered, blended with the sense of wonder of

futures that never were, inspired by the founders of science fiction, all with our own unique spirit of independence with the occasional hint of anarchy. It makes for unbridled creativity with a touch of the familiar."

Performance personas are worked into music, making, and fashion design. These steamsonas are performed at conventions, role-playing games, and other events. Many creators who aren't actors suddenly acquire stage selves and subculture names, like Jake von Slatt and the late Datamancer, or the musicians Captain Robert of Abney Park, Mr. B the Gentleman Rhymer, and Doctor Steel (the originator of the catchphrase that serves as this sidebar's title). Theater in Steampunk can be as top-notch as professional productions of Shakespeare using the industrial motif. Or it can be as simple as players in a live-action role-playing game, such as the well-known Steam & Cinders from Massachusetts.

More than your average cosplayer is a creator like Justin Stanley, an assemblage artist who also does performance work. Stanley describes his art as "taking puzzle pieces of someone's past and forming them together to create a window into another world." As the "Emperor Justinian Stanislaus," Stanley rules the Multiverse against the DULL. "Using imagination and creativity is the source of truly enjoying life," he explains. The Emperor also runs the Red Fork Empire, which is a real-life artist collective as opposed to an oppressive regime.

The lightheartedness of Steampunk inspired activist Miriam Rosenberg Roček to create her Steampunk persona, Emma Goldman, based on the historical Russian Jewish anarchist. "Part of what I'm always trying to do is make politics and history more fun and entertaining," says Roček, "and by putting in Steampunk, it is reassuring people that they are not looking for something too serious or academic." As Steampunk Emma Goldman, Roček has led political rallies at conventions to spread awareness, and she puts "your politics into your Steampunk, and your Steampunk into your politics" using her blog and Facebook page.

Steampunk opens the way for innovative storytelling methods as well. The League of S.T.E.A.M., a transmedia production company, does live shows, runs an award-winning web series, and manages the Jr. League W.A.T.C.H., an interactive fan club. "I like to describe [our work] as live shows using close-up magic with technology as opposed to trickery," explains Glenn Freund, one of the members in this popular troupe. He started off as a hobbyist, but over the years he now considers himself an art-

ist because of the League. To Freund, the difference between these labels is how an artist gains a sense of focus: "[the] act and energy into what you're doing [versus] understanding the consequence of the art you're doing." The League inspired other people to do similar work worldwide; the newest organization of this type is the Adventurers League of G.E.A.R.S. artists' collective in New Orleans.

Yomi Ayeni, producer of the transmedia event Clockwork Watch in London, agrees that this type of interactive platform-jumping gives everyone the capability to believe in their artistic selves. "Life is a multifaceted world, and the things that you share are deeply personal: A woman who gets off of a bus and is given a rose may think the world is beautiful, a man who stepped out of a movie theater may suddenly see the world as cosmic. . . . We want each aspect of the story that people bring to create some positive difference," Ayeni says. During our Skype interview, he gushed about Haley Moore of Laser Lace Letters as an example. Moore had written stories set in the Clockwork Watch universe, and she became so inspired by her art for Clockwork Watch that she quit her job to become a full-time maker and independently crowd-sourced more than $17,000 to set up her own business. She is currently writing a six-part spin-off series that Clockwork Watch will publish.

Spaces for art and performance aren't limited to the stage, either: even a hotel can suffice. Just ask Eric Larson, aka Lord Hastings Robert Bobbins, whose directorial method of running Wisconsin-based TeslaCon turns a convention into a theatrical experience. In TeslaCon's "immersive" environment, people can come and play in TeslaCon's world as their own characters. "People are able to explore a part of themselves, albeit with a character or invented person that they usually wouldn't do in public that they feel okay doing here at the convention," Larson observes. Steampunk isn't only about the costuming, according to him, but the personality that can come out of the clothing. There, hallways and lobbies are transformed into interiors of submarines and rocket ships. A staff of professional actors (and some life-sized puppets!) facilitates an ongoing, four-year story line. Films let audiences travel to the moon or fight underwater battles. In this world that is more than make-believe, Larson says, "Attendees are able to express themselves in ways that make them grow as a person."

The capability of opening the imagination to create stronger human connections is another lasting impact of Steampunk performance. The League of S.T.E.A.M., for example, has done shows at Disneyland, the Electronic Entertainment Expo, and even at a private event of two hundred billionaires. No matter from what background, Steampunk catches people's attention. "People are first curious, excited, and entertained. Our work is tangible disbelief," says Freund. "It's all plausible enough for people to enjoy it."

Roček notices how her informal acting establishes a shared love for an extraordinary historical figure. "I've had people write to me with personal stories about Emma, or even say, 'I'm visiting the Haymarket and thought of you,' or 'I left a rose on your grave.' People have things that they wish to say to her, and I think sometimes, on a good day, my character provides an outlet for that."

Velazquez recounted the story of one man who suffers from chronic pain and rarely left the house before he and his wife started attending the Artifice Club's Mechanical Masquerade, and he looks forward to those minutes on the dance floor when he can be together with her. "What I work on, and what my team helps plan and run, provides hope for someone and something to look forward to."

What Steampunk objects and performances have in common, then, is that both contain an effusive outpouring of creative excess that brings people together. The physicality of Steampunk is reinforced by performance: By dealing with the materials, people touch the immaterial parts of themselves, the bonds of a community. Hope and new possibilities become symbolized by the objects Steampunks cherish and construct. This is more than simple beauty, but the meaning of art itself.

Larson makes this point most succinctly: "I see Steampunk creation as a whole interconnected system, where different art forms cannot be sectioned off from each other. The makers are influenced by the designers; the designers, the mechanics; the mechanics, the dressmakers; the dressmakers back to the modders. That's how it works."

That is why, to many Steampunk creators, Steampunk isn't only a "look" but also a mode of being, a state of creativity that draws upon both the darkness and the light of the past to try to create an imagined utopic space in the present day. Performance and queer studies scholar José Esteban Muñoz—not a Steampunk, but certainly one of the academic inspirations behind this article, and my late mentor—believed in the power that is embodied in a range of performances from drag shows to theater; we once talked about Steampunk in this light, too. Muñoz wrote about the importance of these performances as being extraordinary visions of new futures evoked against today's drab, imperfect world: "The here and now is a prison house. We must strive, in the face of the here and now's totalizing rendering of reality, to think and feel a then and there. Some will say that all we have are the pleasures of the moment, but we must never settle for that minimal transport; we must dream and enact new and better pleasures, other ways of being in the world, and ultimately new worlds." Likewise, Steampunk performance reaches for something greater than the sum of its parts— the dream of a more fascinating, beautiful, and wondrous reality.

....

Diana M. Pho is a scholar, editor, activist, and performer. In the Steampunk community, she is known as Ay-leen the Peacemaker and runs *Beyond Victoriana*, the award-winning blog on multicultural Steampunk. She also has a master's degree in performance studies from New York University, where her final project focused on using Steampunk as an empowering storytelling vehicle for marginalized people.

Finding the Path to Steampunk

Are Steampunk musicians born or made? Perhaps a little of both. Though Steampunk music and performance remains a niche, for many of the artists we talked to, it was simply the most natural expression of their interests and experiences.

Take Voltaire. A longtime staple of the Steampunk scene, Voltaire is a multitasking Renaissance man whose creative output includes songwriting and musical performances, a career in stop-motion animation, a comic book series that was developed by Syfy into a fourteen-episode animated web series (written and directed by Voltaire himself), and even a foray into toy making. His music falls under the auspices of dark cabaret, or, according to his current bio, "a collection of murder ballads, tongue-in-cheek exercises in the macabre, with just enough bawdy songs about *Star Trek* and *Star Wars* to keep a convention audience rolling in the aisles."

ABOVE
Voltaire works on stop-motion animation for his film *Odukuro*. Photo credit: Voltaire.
OPPOSITE
Voltaire and his merry band of Steampunk pirates. Photo credit: Voltaire.

For someone so multitalented and creatively inclined, perhaps the gravitation toward Steampunk was inevitable. Voltaire says, "I've always loved the macabre, the gothic, science fiction, horror, fantasy, pageantry, the antiquated and elegant. I suppose it stands to reason that whatever I create will be informed by these things I love. The beauty of being inspired by many, sometimes disparate, things, is that the art you create in turn could potentially be a very new or unique melding of different influences; a new recipe using existing ingredients, if you will."

For Shelby of the Cassettes, Victoriana served as an early reference point. He says, "I've always been attracted to imagery of early transportation and the imaginings of Jules Verne and H. G. Wells. . . . At a point in 2003, the Cassettes took a more roots-music turn and it felt right to begin to explore those 'Steampunk' themes with our music and imagery."

Crystal Bright, front woman of the "kaleidophrenic cabaret" act Crystal Bright and the Silver Hands, grew into her unique, eclectic sound by way of a surprisingly circuitous journey around the world. "There was not one single path that led me to the music and art I create now, but many. I've always been interested in other cultures and their music, especially the Roma, and I went on to study anthropology and ethnomusicology, which expanded my knowledge and interests even more." She's played with a wide variety of musical ensembles, drawing on such diverse influences as mariachi, Ugandan, Chinese, and Brazilian music. She's studied salsa, flamenco, and West African dance. She even plays the accordion and the concertina, an Argentinean drum, and an Ugandan harp.

Sunday Driver is another band with a particularly eclectic blend of influences, an exciting fusion of classical Indian music and English folk. Like many, Sunday Driver stumbled into Steampunk by happy accident, through interests both aesthetic and political. "We were kind of 'doing' Steampunk before we realized it existed as a genre. Our first album, *In the City of Dreadful Night,* was inspired by thinking about cities—particularly Calcutta and London—in Victorian times. We conjured up apocalyptic scenes of poverty and squalor—things people wouldn't normally talk about or sing about but which existed behind all the decadence and grandeur. Our songs touched on vermin, whorehouses, opium dens, and other such delights. It was an attempt to expose the hypocrisy in how history is told."

Sunday Driver worked to realize this vision through their entire act, drawing on visual aspects such as costumes and stage sets. The approach, however, elicited confusion from some of their viewers. "Most people didn't know what to make of us when we turned up to play in indie music venues—why was the guitarist performing in a dirty old turban? Why was the clarinet player in a rather immodest corset?" Then, one day, the band turned up to play at an event billed as Steampunk . . . and found an incredibly receptive audience. "They just seemed to *get* our music and what we were doing without needing any explanation. It felt like coming home."

Steampunk Music's Past and Future:
Steering Clear of Clichés

Despite its inclusive categories, Steampunk music—particularly those bands that self-identify as such—can also be a somewhat insular community, riffing on an increasingly self-referential set of material. As a result, there are certain genre conventions that have become a little too familiar to those in the Steampunk scene.

Abney Park is one of today's longest-running Steampunk acts; they staked their claim when Steampunk was still a wild, woolly, and unfamiliar frontier. As a result, they are probably the best-known Steampunk band today, or at least one of the first names that comes to mind. They have observed Steampunk's steady rise over the past decade or so, and all the changes that an exponential growth in popularity has brought to the scene.

Many of those have been wonderful changes, but some have also been less welcome; for example, Abney Park member Robert expressed frustration with the ways in which Steampunk has become a commodity. "I'm fairly annoyed by people dressing Steampunk, then making music with zero vintage in the sound, and calling themselves Steampunk music makers," he says. "There are also a ton more clones these days. Cosplayers playacting they are Steampunks in a hotel lobby. People, instead of being their own original interpretation on Steampunk, show up looking almost identical to everyone else."

Compared to Abney Park, the Clockwork Dolls are a much newer addition to the scene. Their first album, *Dramatis Personae*, is a richly narrative work set in a "neo-Victorian Steampunk universe." Their second album, however, pushes into retro-futurist territory that is decidedly less well trod; inspired by the era of World War II, *When Banners Fall* is described by the band as "a tribute to our greatest generation in their darkest hour." Despite the different approaches in their work, the Clockwork Dolls' composer and keyboardist Allison Curval agrees with Abney Park's take on Steampunk music clichés; she says, "I would love—and I know people will kill me for talking about this—to see less of an emphasis on just playing music with goggles on your hats and more of an emphasis in creating music that takes its inspiration from history. After all, isn't that a big part of what Steampunk is? The fictional future filtered through the imagination of the past?"

But for the most part, musicians seem to take a pretty tolerant attitude toward Steampunk clichés. For example, the Mechanisms, another folk-inspired cabaret act that incorporates spirited storytelling into their boisterous performances, playacting futuristic fairy tales as portrayed by Steampunk space pirates. They spoke up on behalf of conventions: "First, we'd like to say we're really uncomfortable with being disparaging about clichés. Tropes and clichés are not in themselves a bad thing. We don't want to say that, for instance, goggles are clichéd, and have that come across as our saying 'Don't wear goggles.' Apart from anything else, that would be wildly hypocritical, given how many of us own goggles!"

The important thing is feeling free to experiment, neither beholden to convention nor determined to flout it. "What is more of a problem than clichés themselves is people feeling constrained by clichés," the Mechanisms add. "Tropes and clichés aren't bad, but it's important to have the freedom

to play with them, and to recognize that there is space under the 'Steampunk' label for people who embrace them, people who want to subvert them or use them in unusual ways, and people who avoid them in favor of less commonly explored areas."

One interesting musical act currently exploring the far edges of subversion is the Men That Will Not Be Blamed for Nothing. Their rather unwieldy name is a reference to a scrawled line of enigmatic graffiti attributed by some to Jack the Ripper, the mysterious serial killer who terrorized London in the late 1880s. Vocal-

ist and guitarist Andy Heintz also emphasized the diversity of Steampunk music, which has just as much room for a raucous, abrasive, and bitingly comedic band like the Men That Will Not Be Blamed for Nothing. "I don't think anything is clichéd in Steampunk music, simply because there is no particular sound you can point at and call Steampunk—it's more to do with attitude, visual style, and lyrical subject matter," he says, adding, "Every Steampunk band approaches the music from their own direction, and there is room in the scene for all of us, from Abney Park's cosplay world of sky pirates, through the whimsy of Professor Elemental's chap-hop, to our filthy Victorian Whitechapel punk underclass."

Steampunk Music's Past and Future:
Pursuing the New

So what does the future hold for Steampunk music and perfor-mance? Hopefully, lots more experimentation and innovation, with a generous dose of mad invention and social change.

"It would be great if more Steampunk artists would write less for a genre and more from their own personal creativity and inspiration," observes Crystal Bright. "I personally would love to see more instruments like my own being used, such as accor-dion, saw, and other acoustic instruments, because if that apoca-lypse that Steampunk refers to a lot comes, and we have limited sources of power, then the show will go on!"

The Cassettes, a self-described "mystic country" band, are an inventive and original group that tends to skirt the bound-ary between vaudevillian Steampunk and scrappy indie rock. With an eye toward Steampunk music's future, front man Shelby Cinca tells us, "I'd like to see more explorations in the rhythms of locomotives, music with minimal or no electricity, to really engage the thoughts of an alternate 'Steampunk' retro-future and what that would be inspired from, with less of the 'Hollywood' aspects." He adds, "I think, ethically, I'd love to see a more 'punk' approach to it all—booking shows in barns, Victorian mansions, etc. . . . breaking out of the sci-fi/fantasy conventions and rock club thing."

Speaking of that "punk" approach, the Men That Will Not Be Blamed for Nothing focus less on Steampunk's musical future and more on its untapped potential as a political movement. According to Andy Heintz, Steampunk is still mired in some of the especially problematic aspects of the Victorian era, at times supporting rather than subverting. "Steampunk as a whole tends to fetishize the upper classes, aristocracy, and military—we want to redress the balance. In the words of Occupy, we are the ninety-nine percent," says Andy. "Victorian society was a horrible, racist, sexist, violent, sick place, and pretending to be Lord This or Lady That denies that real-ity. The most interesting and inspiring people of those times actually hated being Victorians and all the rules and etiquette that society forced on them. We want to celebrate the underdogs, the workers, and the misfits, but also use the Victorian era as an allegory to comment on the present."

Perhaps there's a reason why Steampunk feels so politically relevant to this day and age, as comments Max of the Absinthe Drinkers. "Steam-punk's preoccupation with Victorianism and the Gilded Age is interesting, considering that we are in a sort of second Gilded Age right now," he says. "Just as today, great scientific advancements and mind-boggling wealth went hand in hand with terrible inequality and a political system still mud-dling to adapt to these new conditions. I think that the Victorian/Gilded Age speaks to us because people then were so fascinated and appalled by their own modernity, rather the way we are by our own gains and failures."

DIY for Musicians and Performers

The do-it-yourself impulse manifests itself in the maker's fascination with technology that can be taken apart and tinkered with (and hopefully put back together again), and the cosplayer's commitment to crafting a gorgeous costume from bits and scraps. But does the DIY ethic apply to musical acts, too? The answer is a resounding, enthusiastic *YES*.

For example, Abney Park says, "Everything we do is DIY. Nothing we use onstage is unadorned. Our studio is fully Steampunk, from floor to ceiling. Our outfits are all handmade. We ourselves do nearly everything that goes into our albums, and anything we 'farm out' we are really just employing our friends to do."

"DIY is paramount for us," agree the Men That Will Not Be Blamed for Nothing. "We do everything ourselves—from organizing our gigs and tours to recording and releasing records and making merchandise. We produce fanzines and encourage others to do things and make things for themselves. (We released two wax cylinders of songs along with instructions on how to make an 'Edison-style' player to play them on, for example.) This is why we feel so at home in the Steampunk scene."

And, for some performers, DIY extends beyond the art of set design or the business of marketing and promotion into the more technical aspects of music making itself. Shelby Cinca offers up the Cassettes' own thereminist as an example: "Our thereminist has been working on sequences and theremins since the eighties," says Cinca. "He creates his own designs and sells them online. . . . It is his life's work to perfect his theremin designs and it is just what drives him in his creativity."

FINDING INSPIRATION

Tips from Musicians and Performers

Where do Steampunk-style musicians and performers find their ideas? Everywhere! As Malcom from the Unextraordinary Gentlemen comments, "Inspiration is the name of the universe"—and the sources that inspire creativity are wild, joyous, and diverse. So open your eyes, and your ears!

"Comics inspire me a lot, as do long journeys and my ridiculous children. Beyond that, it is mostly conversations that help turn ideas into songs— ideally those late-night CONVERSATIONS with close friends that end with the words 'Well, you could never do a SONG about that.'"

—*Professor Elemental*

"Movies, TV, and books. Spending time away from music and living life tends to RECHARGE the batteries. I tend to not be creative if I just sit there and say, 'I'm going to write a song today.'"

—*Richard, Unextraordinary Gentlemen*

"I always say that I'm inspired by mediocrity and garbage. SERIOUSLY. When I turn on the radio or a TV and I'm appalled by what passes as 'art,' I have a dialogue with myself. It generally consists of me telling myself that I'm probably not the best musician, or filmmaker, or author, but that I could probably do better than what I've just seen. It inspires me to create. It gives me the confidence to *try.*"

—*Voltaire*

"I'm inspired by my life. As *traumatic* THINGS happen, I tend to try to put them into little METAPHORICAL stories to help me deal with them."

—*Robert, Abney Park*

"Stories, I love stories. Stories flesh out our lives and give our experiences context. They also make writing a song a visceral experience. Without a narrative there can be no product. That's the serious answer. . . . The other answer is video games. I play a lot of VIDEO games."

—*Allison, Clockwork Dolls*

"I am inspired by characters, archetypes, and great stories. I want to go on journeys, and I want to take beautiful people with me. I want to live these stories and I don't want to do it alone. I need people to *come with me*, and I need my STORY to be good enough that they will want to. I need to share, and I need to give. I was put on this earth to serve. I know this. I love this. Share with me your ears, your eyes, your time, and I will give you the world. I'll even make you a whole new world. That's all I need."

—*Emilie Autumn*

OPPOSITE ABOVE
On the set of Professor Elemental's *I'm British* video shoot. Photo by Ben Broomfield.
OPPOSITE BELOW
The Mechanisms. Photo by Curious Magpie Photography.

The Art of Found-Percussion

by Eric Farber

ABOVE
The Red Oak Suitcase (collapsed) by Eric Farber. Photo by Dani Leventhal.

OPPOSITE
Eric Farber posing with his work *Batterie-en-Valise: music for two percussionists and five suitcases.* Photo by Dani Leventhal.

I am a percussionist. Lots of percussionists perform music that was composed entirely by someone else (often someone whom they've never met, and more likely still, someone who hasn't celebrated their own birthday in a few centuries). These types of percussionists have their complete parts transcribed in meticulous detail on many pages of paper that they carefully monitor and respond to accordingly, always obliging the frantic, baton-wielding traffic cop that gestures from a center-stage podium.

I have never been one of those types of percussionists.

I spent my teenage years (the 1990s) playing a variety of popular musical styles in suburban basements and garages, took a wrong turn into a conservatory jazz program that lacked forward thinking, found myself in the middle of a bustling arts community in the Lower East Side of Manhattan (replete with absinthe-fueled, orgiastic happenings, operating out of the then-multitude of abandoned spaces in the area), and worked as a burlesque drummer—alongside graceful contortionists and sword-swallowing comedians—for nearly a decade; it was perhaps the twenty-first-century equivalent of joining the circus.

Feeling constrained by my store-bought, mass-produced musical equipment, in 2007 I began experimenting with an array of found objects. I've heard that necessity is the mother of invention, and around that time I found myself in creative musical situations that begged for a more diverse collection of sounds than my typical assortment of drums, cymbals, and standard auxiliary percussion could supply.

I had recently joined the Brooklyn-based indie-vaudeville band the Lisps, and the contributing songwriter—César Alvarez—and I were dig-

Pennsylvania by Eric Farber, built in collaboration with the American Repertory Theater, Cambridge, MA. Photo by Dani Leventhal.

ging through his father's collection of rusty tools in the garage of his parents' house in Yonkers, New York, searching for something that we felt was missing from one of the tracks off of our nearly completed debut full-length album—*Country Doctor Museum.*

We were unable to specify exactly what we were looking for, but recognized that the current state of the percussion sounds on the rowdy song "The Familiar Drunk" were too conventional to match the whiskey-induced auctioneer-paced lyrics, and the woozy, irreverent vocal melody. Buried in an abandoned corner of the garage was an empty two-door filing cabinet. We also discovered a collection of large monkey wrenches, and a few other nameless, dust-covered items. Banging on the thin steel top of the filing cabinet with the heavy monkey wrenches produced a unique cavernous thud that complemented the recording nicely, and which ultimately became integrated in the Lisps' live performances. This experiment sparked my interest in the creative process of bricolage—the generating of work from components that happen to be available or accessible at the time.

Since then I have done a great deal of collecting and tinkering, developing a unique arsenal of *found-percussion,* which I employ in a multitude of contexts. I built a series of large, manually powered percussion machines for the Lisps' sci-fi Civil War musical *FuTURITY* (in collaboration with the American Repertory Theater, Cambridge, MA). Juxtaposing decaying remains of mechanized industry, these hand-cranked "drum machines" play a series of melodies upon activation—a forgotten flywheel becomes a giant music box; a Victorian sewing machine treadle plays a melody on a pair of spinning art deco film reels.

For the Foundry Theatre's 2013 production of Bertolt Brecht's *Good Person of Szechwan* (which appeared at La MaMa and the Public Theater in New York City), I created a portable assemblage of percussive found objects which are mounted to the inside of a wood-framed attaché case from the mid-1960s. The briefcase flips open and its contents get played while it rests on my lap. Enjoying the challenge and value of building such assemblages tailored to the inside dimensions of an existing space, I built five more cases with various percussive purposes, and composed a series of music for a new original project—*Batterie-en-Valise: music for two percussionists and five suitcases.*

This type of work is intrinsically tied to the act of happening upon objects and materials, since much of what I use is not regularly stocked at a local retailer, but is found farther out on the fringes. A certain amount of "luck" (which involves some mix of access, learned skill, intuition, and literal dumb luck) plays a huge role in the outcome of these projects, as it determines the materials that I will work with. Also required is a creative imagination, within which I can play with an object that I may come across, and wonder about its potential, while considering the context of other objects or projects I may already have.

I began this writing describing a certain relationship between composers and musicians, and considering where I fit into that equation. Many composers start their work with a certain sound, melody, or concept in mind, and then set out to find the appropriate instrumentation—whether conventional musical instruments or objects that are less standard—to satisfy their demands. I tend to take an opposite approach.

I'd like to think that my projects represent a collaboration between myself and the objects that I work with. An object's formal qualities—to what extent it is resonant, mountable, functional, etc.—is the greatest factor in determining the way the pieces come together structurally, and the music that is ultimately generated from the assemblages. Approaching an object by considering its potential to perform reliably in some way, while conjuring a certain respect for it as an autonomous object with its own historical reality, has been the closest thing to a formula that I have developed for asking an object about how it wants to be involved in my project of making music.

....

Eric Farber has lived in Brooklyn, New York, since 2004. His "found-percussion" assemblages have been featured in a number of regional and off-Broadway theater productions, including the Foundry Theatre's *Good Person of Szechwan*, and *Futurity: A Musical by The Lisps*. See Eric's work at www.kineticontology.com.

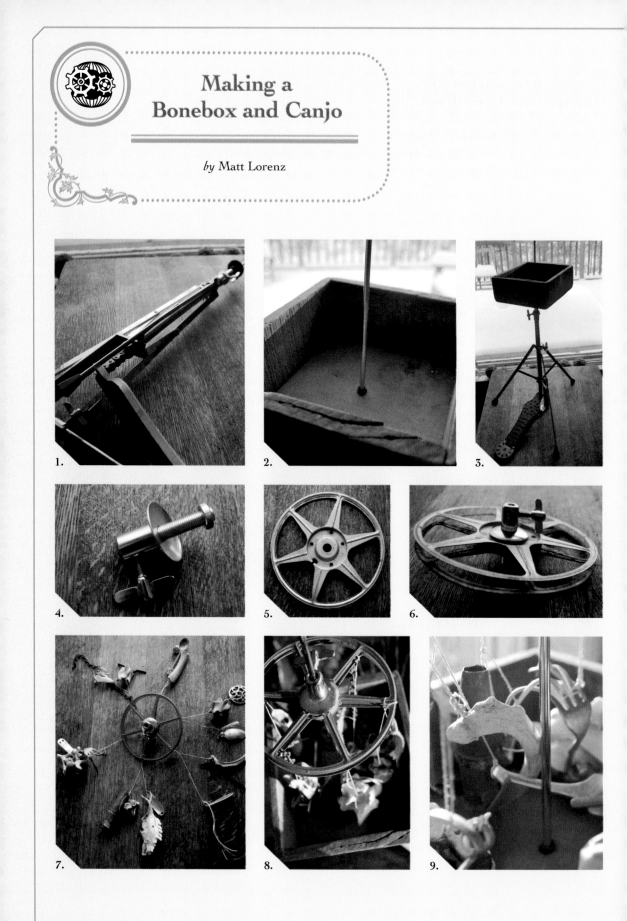

Making a Bonebox and Canjo

by Matt Lorenz

1.

2.

3.

4.

5.

6.

7.

8.

9.

Inspired to try your own DIY project? In this next piece, musician and performer Matt Lorenz demonstrates how he created two offbeat musical instruments from found materials. The first—the "bonebox"—is a percussion instrument similar to a wind chime, created from an unlikely source. The second is a banjo-like instrument made from a tin can, leading to the obvious moniker "canjo."

Part I: Making the Bonebox

I'm the type of person who collects bones, old silverware, and odd little items that seem to have life in them. For the longest time, this ever-growing collection cluttered my shelves and drawers, occasionally overflowing and finding its way into some kind of sculpture project. Recently, I was searching for sounds for the Suitcase Junket (my one-man band) and dropped a box of bones on the floor. It sounded great, so I decided to do something about it. Here's a play-by-play.

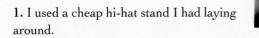

1. I used a cheap hi-hat stand I had laying around.

2, 3. I found a nice old box (I like the sound of wood, but metal would probably be interesting, too) and drilled a hole in the middle of it the size of the hi-hat stand where it will sit. Then I set the box onto the stand.

4. The clutch for the hi-hat stand is what usually holds the top cymbal and attaches it to the rod that moves up and down.

5. I decided on an old 8mm film reel to act as my "top cymbal."

6. Attaching the clutch to the film reel can be tricky. Some fit quite nicely, but you may have to widen the hole in the reel with a drill bit.

7. Next, I tied all the trinkets, doodads, and whatnots to the reel, trying to keep the weight balanced.

8, 9. Lastly, I put the clutch and reel onto the hi-hat stand and experimented with height. I set mine so that most of the pieces are just barely touching the box or are floating slightly above it. It sounds like a little tiny troop of marching marionettes. I intend to make more of these with different sets of objects, as I still have a lot of detritus kicking around in my room.

Part II: Making the Canjo

1. Here are some things you will need in order to make a canjo:
A can (the size and shape of which will determine the sound you get), a sturdy piece of wood such as a broom handle (this will be the neck and fingerboard), a guitar or banjo string, an awl (anything that can poke a hole through metal will do), some pliers, an eye hook, and a random object that will serve as a bridge. (I prefer teeth, a nicely shaped bone, or that particular piece of curtain rod hardware that holds the rod to the window frame.)

2. Lay the wood across the middle of the closed end of the can and mark just below the can's lip the approximate size of the wood. Make your marks slightly smaller than the wood. This will make for a more snug fit later on.

3. Poke a hole in the middle of the marked spots.

4. Use the pliers to widen the small holes to just under the size of your wood. This is fairly easily done by pushing and twisting the pliers into the can. (Do be careful with the edges of the metal, as they are sharp and will draw blood.)

5. You should now have two holes directly across from each other just under the closed end of the can.

6. Insert the wood handle and work it through both holes.

7. Twisting back and forth as you push usually works nicely and makes a fine little design as well. Leaving the two holes slightly smaller than the wood makes it so the can itself is holding the wood in place so there is no need for extra hardware.

8. Starting to look like an instrument already!

9. I forgot to mention that you will need a drill of some kind and a drill bit. The bit should be larger than the string but smaller than the ball at the end of the string. This hole here is in what you'd call the tailpiece.

10. This next hole is to be drilled on the other end, in the headstock.

11. The third hole is a pilot hole. It goes about halfway through and should be an inch or two above the other hole in the headstock on the backside of the neck. This is where the eye hook will be screwed in. Without a pilot hole, the eye hook will most likely split the wood.

12. Screw in the eye hook just a few turns.

13. Insert the string up through the hole in the tailpiece . . .

1.

2.

3.

4.

5.

6.

7.

8.

9.

10.

11.

12.

13.

14. Then down through the hole in the headstock.

15. Tie the string to the eye hook using a double granny knot. (Instead of looping the string through once, do it twice.)

16, 17. Using a nail to tighten the eye hook spares your fingers and gives you some mechanical advantage.

18. In choosing a bridge, there are a couple of things to keep in mind. First, it needs to be tall enough to lift the string above the lip of the can. (Sometimes I hammer down the edge of the can so as to have more leeway for the string.) Second, the bridge is what transfers the sound from the string to the can bottom. Different materials/objects very much control the sound of the instrument. I recommend experimenting with different things. In my experience, tooth and bone do a good job of this, but metal and wood have their own interesting sounds as well.

19.

19. Picks can be made from just about anything. Bouncing the tuning nail on the string sounds pretty good, too. If you like a slide sound, I recommend using a bottle neck or a knife, and if you want to try bowing the string and don't have a violin bow, try unwaxed dental floss strung between the ends of a bent sapling branch. (You will need a lot of rosin on the bow strings if you try this. It can be bought at almost any music store.)

....

Matt Lorenz is a compulsive creator of sights and sounds. He hails from the Connecticut River Valley in Vermont and Massachusetts and can often be found touring with the Suitcase Junket (his one-man band; www.the suitcasejunket.com) or Rusty Belle (a sibling trio; www.rustybelle.com). You can see more of Lorenz's projects at www.makingwhatiwant.com.

Learning the Basics: The Steampunk Musician's Tools

Just as fortune favors the prepared, DIY rewards the diligent. Luckily, it's a self-reinforcing cycle; the more you do it yourself, the more you learn. And the more you learn, the more successful your DIY projects will be.

That's not to say it will always be easy. At one point or another, every creative person faces a gap between the limits of their ability and the reaches of their ambition; the trick is working through it. "My difficulty from the very start has always been trying to express myself onstage and tell my stories within the limitations of essentially having a budget of ten dollars, and with a creative staff of exactly one person—me," comments Emilie Autumn. "I've always wanted more tools at my creative disposal, naturally, and have worked every day from the beginning toward building those tools."

So how do you learn the basics? And what can an aspiring musician do to expand the tools at their disposal? For César Alvarez of the Lisps, the learning process involved: "School. Reading. Making work. Putting my work onstage even though it wasn't quite ready. Asking successful people to speak with me about their work. After failing and being rejected numerous times, just keep going."

Amour Obscur is a Brooklyn-based band with a retro-futurist sound that *New York* magazine termed "Weimar punk"; their influences include traditional Romany music and 1920s Berlin cabaret. (In fact, singer Dee Dee Vega's past experience includes performing in a contemporary cabaret in Berlin.) The band beefed up their skills and logged their practice hours together, using a method that's a bit unusual in this day and age: busking.

It makes sense, considering they live in Brooklyn, where it's not uncommon for buskers to set up shop on busy blocks, in tourist-heavy parks, and

on crowded subway platforms. "Busking is an excellent way of streamlining your performance," says the band's accordion player, Matt Dallow. "When I started busking, I would busk alone, and I would play most of my repertoire, then figure out what songs made me the most money, and I'd play them over and over again. When recording Amour Obscur's upcoming album, our single 'Berlin, Your Dance Partner Is Death' was only recently written, and as we performed it more and more, it changed a little bit, not majorly, but little glissandos and fills and whatnot were added to showcase transitions and the next sections. . . . I call this the marination period of a song. . . . It's like how a play is so much more powerful and exciting after the first week."

"Like with anything, it's just a lot of practice, discipline, and having the drive to keep going," concludes Richard of the Unextraordinary Gentlemen. "Plus, it helps to know people who are doing what you want to do and learn from them. Also, we get by with a little help from our friends."

It's true; the Steampunk community is a particularly supportive one. Chances are, if you need a little help or guidance, all you have to do is ask.

ABOVE
Amour Obscur. Photo by Tod Seelie.

The Creative Life: A Working Process for Musicians and Performers

So. You have your grand idea. You have an idea of what *your sound* sounds like. And you aren't half bad on the harmonica. What comes next? How do you turn a whistled couple of notes or a fragment of a lyric into a finished song? Well, César Alvarez of the Lisps broke down his working process for us like this:

Have idea. > Look up on Internet. > Read Wikipedia. > Read books. > Watch videos. > Write songs. > Apply for grants. > Get rejected. > Put on show anyway. > Invite friends. > Pay bills somehow. > Repeat.

More seriously, most musical acts—especially those with two or more members—have a process that involves both solitary and collaborative brainstorming. Typically, musicians make a point of recording those fleeting, random bursts of inspiration, whether by writing down the lyrics, transcribing the musical notes, or recording themselves as they play the tune. Then they bring these pieces to the group and work together to flesh the fragments out into a full-length song. (A solo performer often has a similar process, except instead of setting aside time to brainstorm with bandmates, they devote a specific time to working in a focused way; this time is distinct from more flexible periods of unfocused creative noodling.) Once they have a working song, they play it through a few times and allow it to evolve naturally and organically.

Research can also play a role, especially for performers with a more narrative approach to songwriting. Take, for example, when the Clockwork Dolls were putting together their World War II–influenced album, *When Banners Fall*. Composer Allison Curval took her research duties for this project seriously: "I did research as far as immersing myself in the cultural landscape of the period. I listened to a lot of newsreels, old-time radio, speeches from the leaders of the time, and at one point even tried to ration myself appropriately (it didn't go so well)." She believes this kind of work is essential: "I think historical research is *vital* for anyone interested even on the superficial level of going into Steampunk or any sort of retro-futurism, because it's the framework that one builds upon," she says.

While implementing an Industrial Age diet may be a bit extreme, there is no doubt that every creative team has its own little quirks. Whether for an individual artist or a collaborative group, there are certain practices that signal "Okay, it's time to work." When you hit on one of these talismanic symbols or Pavlovian practices, it's best to go with the flow. For Amour Obscur, the creative process includes holing up together in singer Dee Dee's apartment "for an evening with a handle of Evan Williams and her weird little dog." Robert of Abney Park likes to spend rainy days in the studio, going through notes and turning the fragments of inspiration into songs. And Kat from Sunday Driver says, "I don't want to give away too many of our secrets, but I can tell you it involves a lot of tea."

One thing is evident: Our accomplished musicians and performers rely heavily on their creative beverage of choice. So pick your poison—whether it be a bottle of whiskey, a pot of tea, or a historically appropriate glass of absinthe—and settle down to brainstorm.

Collaboration with the Band

As evidenced by the previous section, collaboration is often a critical aspect of the creative process, especially for musical acts. Of course, when you get together a bunch of talented people with an ambitious goal, an assortment of instruments, and quite possibly a big pot of tea, there is plenty of energy to fuel the creative process—and, occasionally, a few obstacles to slow it down.

On the one hand, having a large group comprised of different personalities makes it easier to work through creative challenges, and solve them; there are lots of advantages when it comes to heavy-duty brainstorming or tackling a variety of responsibilities. On the other hand, visions can conflict, and compromise can be a slow and sticky process. But collaboration also has its rewards.

Robert of Abney Park commented on one advantage: never having to shoulder the burden of invention alone. "Occasionally even the most prolific artists will get stuck on songs," says Robert. "Having a small army of talented people at your call to help you push a song from 'Eh' to 'Wow!' really helps keep things moving forward."

"What's nice about being together for so long is that we've got used to how we work, and have learned how to harness our creative tensions in a very positive way," says Kat of Sunday Driver. "We used to argue a lot . . . but now we can do it in a way that leads to something great, rather than stropping out to make tea. I think it's a lot like a marriage, but with seven people. You have to learn to give and take, and you get comfortable with each other's quirks, but there's still a big dollop of passion that makes for great sex. Did I say sex? I meant great music."

There are also logistical challenges to achieving creative harmony as a group. It's great having lots of hands on deck for brainstorming sessions,

but those sessions can be hard to schedule—a challenge that increases exponentially as the group grows in size. This is something the Mechanisms have particularly discovered, as "the crew" currently numbers ten, more or less. "There are practical difficulties in getting everyone in the same place at the same time . . . and sometimes with fitting everyone onstage!" But the advantages of having a big group grow exponentially as well: "There's also a lot of diversity of ideas and tastes, which is both a good and a bad thing— we talk over each other and get sidetracked a lot, but in the end we do come up with a far richer and more varied end product than any one or two of us could produce alone."

As the Cassettes' Shelby Cinca comments, "It can definitely be tricky to organize the different types of personalities in a group. Thereminists can be fickle, and tabla players can wander, but in the end it is extremely reward-ing, since, when such a mismatched and ragtag bunch are all onstage sync-ing musically, it is truly beautiful."

When collaboration works, it's magic, and when a group of creatively talented people just *click*, the result is often sublime, producing much more fantastic and original work than any one person could create on their own. The trick is finding the conspirators and co-creators who make your musi-cal heart soar. For Voltaire, that means looking to work with people he truly admires from an artistic perspective. He says, "I like to surround myself with people who do things better than I do. So for instance, in making an album, I have Brian Viglione of the Dresden Dolls play drums, rather than myself. I have Melora Creager of Rasputina play the cello, rather than myself. I could not begin to hold a candle to the abilities these people have. And moreover, their involvement brings ideas to the table that I don't pos-sess. All in all, the final product becomes greater than the sum of its parts when you combine your own ideas and abilities with the ideas and superior skills of virtuosos."

Collaboration with the Audience

For live performers, there is another essential angle to collaboration: the spontaneous give-and-take that occurs between performer and audience. Many performers crave that immediacy and energy. In some instances, it's the shared energy—the electric connection between artist and audience—that enables the most powerful performances.

Emilie Autumn spoke to us about this dynamic, and her evolving attitude toward audience as she's matured in her talent and her career. "When I began writing, recording, and releasing books and albums, I didn't allow anyone to influence my creative process, and that's why I think it worked . . . because everything I put out was so intense and sincere and honest." She worked hard to nurture what she calls the "fuck off" mentality—the decision to place her own creative vision above anyone else's opinion or commentary.

But today, she's more focused on creating live performances than recording albums. "I'm working on turning my book into a Broadway-style musical, and I'm working on the soundtrack (or score) to that musical. So now I think about the audience . . . anyone who will play with me in this game of 'Let's go on a wild adventure together and let's return home completely changed,' and that now influences my creative process. When I'm writing this musical, I'm not just thinking about where the pause between words should be . . . I'm thinking about the audible gasp from the guy in the front row during that pause."

BELOW
Carlton Cyrus Ward as White Rabbit in Third Rail's production of *Then She Fell*. Photo by Darial Sneed.

The musical in question is based on Autumn's autobiographical novel, *The Asylum for Wayward Victorian Girls*. The book, which draws in part on the author's own experiences when she was hospitalized in a psychiatric ward, is illustrated with full-color drawings, paintings, and photography; the multimedia aspect creates an immersive effect, one which Autumn intends to considerably magnify in the musical. "I think that the audience and I agree on our desire to enjoy a complete entertainment experience," she says. "I want to enter another world, and so do they. We all want a sanctuary where we feel like we belong, and you don't build a community or a sanctuary by choosing between music and theater, aural and visual. . . You appeal to

all senses, use everything you have to affect people's emotions, and I feel I am only just getting started in being able to effectively accomplish this. It's *all* important."

In many ways, interactive performance is an uncharted art form, with plenty of room for exploration and innovation. One fascinating show that's currently getting rave reviews is Third Rail Projects' production of *Then She Fell*. This interactive performance draws on surprisingly similar subject matter to Emilie Autumn's *Asylum*; described by its creators as "immersive theater," *Then She Fell* draws on the writings of Lewis Carroll and takes place in an abandoned hospital ward in Brooklyn. (Third Rail Projects' co–artistic director Tom Pearson says, "Steampunk fans may recognize it from our last Steampunk Haunted House in 2011, back when our Wonderland characters were punked out a bit more. We've since recontextualized it within a hospital ward and as an evening-length immersive theater experience, but it still retains a lot of the creepy quality and Victorian patina.")

No more than fifteen audience members are admitted per show; this intimate group is allowed to explore the set room by room, interacting with actors whose roles are based on characters like the Mad Hatter and the Red Queen, and exploring a set that offers hidden treasures and dark conundrums. The experience is a surreal, dreamlike journey through an enigmatic world, where each audience member is in some small way a part of the cast. As of this writing, the show has run for over a year, with more than five hundred performances.

Pearson, who also plays the role of the White Rabbit, is a choreographer, director, performer, and visual artist, so he brings a diverse artistic skill set to the table; multisensory experiences such as *Then She Fell* are an intriguing way to bring all these forms of creative expression together. Pearson says, "I think problem solving is where some of the most creative moments emerge. If you can figure out how to do something that at first does not seem possible, you often find yourself working in new and unexpected ways, and the results can be very fresh and inventive."

Reproduction and Adaptation: A Steampunk Story from Page to Performance

by Nancy Hightower

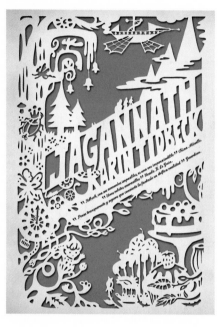

You know the story: Boy meets airship. Boy falls in love with airship. Boy cannot win airship from owner because it is a prototype, so boy orders a copy, which doesn't care for him so much. Boy later meets girl, who is in love with a steam engine. Boy and girl rent a warehouse to shelter both of their mechanical loves, until girl gives birth to baby hybrid steam engine. Mother dies in childbirth, leaving boy and airship as foster parents. Baby hybrid steam engine ends up running away with foster mother airship. And at least two of them live happily ever after.

Karin Tidbeck's story "Beatrice" takes us on the journey of Franz Hiller and Anna Goldberg, both of whom have the misfortune to fall in love with a machine. Their pursuit of these mechanical objects is fueled by earlier fascinations and infatuations. When younger, Anna fell for a Koenig & Bauer printing press, but realized she couldn't follow it everywhere, and so she sets her sights on Hercules, "a round-bellied oven coupled to an upright, broad-shouldered engine. He exuded a heavy aroma of hot iron with a tart overtone of coal smoke that made her thighs tingle."

Franz, on the other hand, cannot quite get over his airship, Beatrice. He encounters her in a Berlin fair, where "She bobbed in a slow up-down motion, like a sleeping whale. But she was very much awake. Franz could feel her attention turn to him and remain there, the heat of her sightless gaze." The owners refuse to sell Beatrice to Franz, since she's a prototype, so he buys a copy of the airship instead.

But once delivered and assembled in the warehouse, Franz senses that this airship does not return his favor the way the original did: "He

summoned the sensation of warm cushions receiving him, how she dipped under his weight. But this Beatrice, Beatrice II, had a seat with firm stuffing that didn't give." Rather than give the airship her freedom, he assures her that "We'll manage. You can be my Beatrice. We'll get used to each other."

While Anna's relationship with Hercules is both satisfying and reciprocal (she constantly feeds him coal), Beatrice II never warms up to Franz's advances and merely tolerates his lovemaking. Anna gives birth to Josephine, a hybrid human with pistons embedded in her skin, but loses her life in the process. Franz becomes Josephine's adoptive father, and it is only when she senses the little one that Beatrice II begins to show any

BELOW
Karin Tidbeck. Photo by
Charlotte Frantzdatter/
Frantzdatter Photography.

interest. The story takes a darker turn once Josephine, who thus far could only sing through her pipes, learns to speak. Because she is a hybrid, at the tender age of four Josephine becomes an interpreter for Beatrice II. The first words that Franz hears Josephine speak, in fact, inform him that the airship's name isn't Beatrice and that "she had lived as a slave" under Franz, "and he had raped her while pretending her to be someone else. She hated him." The one thing the airship wants is to fly. Franz finally allows the airship to leave, and Josephine to escape with her, too.

Tidbeck calls Franz "the tragic hero of his own drama," since it is his own abuse of machines which foretells his separation with his daughter, who is half-machine. The story explores ideas of reproduction, both human and mechanical, as Franz desires an exact replica of his Beatrice, even though her sentience denies such a possibility. He refuses to let the airship do the one thing an airship is supposed to do—fly. Conversely, Anna recognizes her love for the printing press as "an infatuation" and finds a different companion in the steam engine. She also interacts with Hercules as a lover who has physical needs she can fulfill (coal), while also allowing him to fulfill his own mechanistic role (to burn the coal). There is a fascinating interplay between aesthetics and functionality.

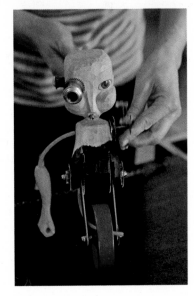

This complex layering makes the story fertile ground for adaptation. The Danish group Tidsrum—which consists of players Ida Marie Tjalve and Karina Nielsen, set designer/puppet builder Sarah Piyannah Cederstrand, dramaturge Sandra Theresa Buch, and composer Andreas Busk—received funding from the Danish Agency for Culture and the Danish Actors' Association to adapt "Beatrice" into a puppet show for children and

young adults. The story begins to morph: A single-author text becomes an orchestra of creative input, provoking plenty of interesting questions along the way. For instance — what kind of background music supports such a piece? "During our workshops we tried out a lot of different music, and we got very fond of some Charleston jazz," says Sarah Cederstrand. "It works very well for the more 'upbeat' scenes, but we also needed something more mechanical."

Enter Andreas Busk, the composer who devised an ingenious, retro-futurist system to capture the subtly haunting aspects of the story: "Basically, we're building two turntables into the stage, to be operated live by the performers. On the first turntable they put specially designed wooden bricks. Each brick has a sound source attached on top of it, in other words, a crystal glass or a copper rod. The second turntable, placed right next to the first, has different mallets installed. When the two turntables spin, the mallets hit the sound sources, creating loops that evolve over time, due to the fact that the turntables run at different speeds. The sounds are picked up via a microphone with a reverb effect that gives all the sounds an abandoned factory–type quality." Busk is still working out the specifics of capturing Josephine's voice, which is both "high and fluting" and yet mechanical because of "a set of minuscule pipes arrayed in her larynx."

Tidsrum's artistic vision also adds new layers to the story; in the early stages of development they discussed using art nouveau and Victorian aesthetics, as they've set the story near 1900. They work with mock-up puppets, testing to see how they need to move, and then dramaturge Sandra Theresa Buch creates them. The puppeteers also have the task of bringing Hercules, the Beatrices, and Josephine to life, to show them in action as characters with feelings and thoughts. "We started looking for references in other art forms such as pictures and books about steam engines, airships, and Victorian technology," Cederstrand says. "We also did some more accurate research on steam engines to be able to design Hercules and Josephine. I had a lot of help from the technical museum in Helsingør, where they have many different machines on display, a lot of books, and a very helpful staff. Andreas and I were lucky to get a grant for a workshop space in a fantastic place, Statens Værksteder for Kunst, where we have access to a fully equipped carpenter's workshop and a metalworking shop. We will be working on the instruments, the set, and the puppets there."

On the other hand, there are still a few practical concerns to work out. Ida Marie Tjalve said she wasn't sure just how they were going to display the sexual interaction between Franz and Beatrice II just yet, "though we did have some rather hilarious tryouts in rehearsals with Franz doing vigorous humping on top of the zeppelin and inside the gondola." Cederstrand, who learned how to make classical Czech marionettes at Puppets in Prague, believes that "the poetic language of puppetry calls for a very strong suspension of disbelief," adding, "when you as the audience accept that the puppets are the characters of the story, it is a much smaller obstacle to accept that they are in love with, and have sex with, living machines."

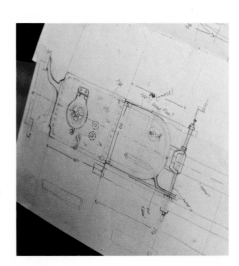

Using shadow play and puppets also creates an immediate and intimate interaction with a collective audience that eludes mechanical capturing. Sure, one can always record the show, and with today's electronics, make it a high-quality film, but the basic tenet of theater is to see it live, to experience the actors (much in the same way that Franz and Anna experience the fairs they attend). While it emphasizes the unique culture of the fair, the performance uses totally low-tech accoutrements; in some ways it might be considered a commentary on the aesthetics of Steampunk itself. Certainly, the process of adaptation, of creating a copy that is as viable as the original, intersects with Franz's own journey from the original Beatrice to the copy he purchases. He never truly embraces the new airship as her own entity, never asks her name, and only assumes the copy is an exact replica of Beatrice. But Beatrice is a sentient being; there can be no true exact copy of her. Had Franz been able to understand the foundations of his infatuation with Beatrice, he might have found love.

It is much the same way with a story and its adaptation. The story is its own living and breathing thing that the reader encounters; while he or she might want or expect a visual performance to replicate the story, it is impossible, because the copy has a life of its own. This makes the creative process all the more exciting, as stories turn and spin, and are even allowed to fly.

....

Nancy Hightower's short fiction and poetry has been published in *Strange Horizons*, *Word Riot*, *storySouth*, *Gargoyle*, *Electric Velocipede*, *Interfictions*, *Prick of the Spindle*, and *Up the Staircase Quarterly*, among others. Her epic fantasy *Elementarí Rising* was published by Pink Narcissus Press in 2013. She is also one of the art columnists for *Weird Fiction Review*.

Seven Pieces of Advice for Aspiring Musicians and Performers

1. "Do it. Start. It will probably be ugly and silly at first. Fine. Keep doing it. **Do your very best. Then DO BETTER. If you're not better after a year or two, maybe do something else.** Pretend you're a rock star or a master painter or a best-selling author if it helps motivate your work, but never despair when those dreams continue to elude you. Do something you love. Somebody else will, too, or maybe they won't. So?"

—*Malcom, Unextraordinary Gentlemen*

2. "Break the idea down into lots of manageable, bite-sized portions. . . . **Also, sometimes the way to *solve problems* is by NOT *thinking about them*.** If I'm stuck with a song, then I know the way to finish it is to walk away from it and let my subconscious do the work."

—*Chandy, Sunday Driver*

3. "**If you want to work with a group, *find* PEOPLE who you can work *with*.** Skills can be learned; belief, trust, and the ability to work together, less so. Everyone involved has to get along, and they have to care. Technical skill is secondary."

—*The Mechanisms*

4. "**Don't make what you think people will like. Make what *you* like.** That's what people will like. We all want to see things which are truth. Truth to the person that made it."

—*The Lisps*

5. "**You need a TEAM of people who SUPPORT you and understand your ideas**—maybe they have similar inspirations or aesthetics—and someone who has great organizational skills, if you don't. But realize you can only truly rely on yourself to get things done. So find the big purposes that lie behind your idea and use those to stabilize and motivate you."

—*Crystal Bright*

6. "Write it down is the best start. **Whatever the idea is, sketch it out on paper, then rewrite it and add more detail.** Then leave it a while and do it again. When you are comfortable that the idea is how it had looked in your head, then you can get on with working out ways to make it into reality."

—*Professor Elemental*

7. "Your slate is never as blank as it seems. **In another reality, everything you DREAM of has already happened, you've already ACHIEVED it, and it was AWESOME. Your only job is to catch up.** And remember that the most beautiful, powerful, honest things you will ever create and give to this world will cost you nothing to produce. Let your big idea be driven by real work on your craft and real-life experience, and nothing can stop you from achieving your vision."

—*Emilie Autumn*

The Afterlife
of the Honey
Bee

RETRO-FUTURE FANTASIES AND STEAMPUNK DREAMS

W hat would you create if time and money were no object? What would you make if all the creative resources you could imagine—not to mention the skills—were at your fingertips? We asked this question of our artists, makers, and creators, encouraging them to get creative (and dream big). We also asked our creators what ultra-ambitious project they'd like to see someone else do. After all, most creators were fans first, and collaborations are rife in Steampunk. Here are some of their niftiest ideas. Some ideas are utterly fantastic; others might just inspire the next big thing.

Big Ideas from Artists and Makers

"I would like to **create a baptism machine to take to Burning Man**. It would be made of glass tubes and joined by metal and rivets. I would like it to release water over the head of the initiated who wish to cleanse their names and refocus their identities. I've performed baptisms for the past few years, and I think it would be striking to have a gleaming, glass machine in the desert."

—*Carrie Ann Baade*

PAGE 232
The Afterlife of the Honeybees by Carrie Ann Baade
ABOVE
Julie by Annliz Bonin
OPPOSITE
Industrial Revolution by John Coulthart

"I'd love to **make a real automated doll**, like the ones I do in photomontage. It would be a full-sized-human scale and fully articulated."

—*Annliz Bonin*

"I would love to **do a stop-motion animated Mechtorians movie** at some point. I don't animate, myself, so I would need to collaborate with a company who I felt understood the characters enough to do them correctly."

—*Doktor A*

"I would really love to **design a set for theater, maybe for a play by Oscar Wilde or Shakespeare**, but give it a retro-futuristic look. A stage is just a big box, after all."

—*Louise Kiner*

QUEEN OF SWORDS

"My ultimate goal is to **create a world that is based on my alternative-history idea** that the Imperial Steamworks imagery has been based on. I want to create an art book that reads like a travel guide to the imperial city in my fantasy world."

—*James Ng*

"I want to **connect** **London and Rio de Janeiro.** This is more tunnel-through-the-earth than pie-in-the-sky, but equally ambitious."

—*Paul St George*

"I'd love to **design a whole game world.** Games are really unparalleled as an experiential and atmospheric medium."

—*Keith Thompson*

"If I were immortal, I'd **finish the all-female art nouveau tarot deck** I started years ago. The way I draw and paint, seventy-two cards would take a long, long time!"

—*Ramona Szczerba*

"I want to **build a thirty-six-foot-tall giant steambot all out of steel, iron, and brass,** standing on my front lawn, posed as if it's attacking my house. I want it to be completely rusted, as if it rusted in place, and I want a death ray on the roof, pointed at the robot, also old, rusted in place, and bro-

ABOVE
Queen of Swords by Ramona Szczerba
OPPOSITE
Harvester by James Ng
OVERLEAF
Serpent Twins, created by Jon Sarriugarte and Kyrsten Mate, and their 'Empire of Dirt' Crew. Design team Because We Can assisted in fabrication and provided additional support.

ken-looking, with a hole burned all the way through the robot, in line with the death ray's sights. I also want a patch of the lawn behind the robot (also in line), made of glass like it had melted the earth behind it, so the whole thing looks like it happened years ago and we just haven't bothered clearing it away."

—*Thomas Willeford*

"I dream of seeing **a Steampunk carousel** one day, and **a zoo** created by Jessica Joslin, and **an insect aviary** created by Mike Libby. Actually, I would love to see a Steampunk circus, filled with automatons and creatures made by the artists that I love."

—*Annliz Bonin*

"**A working, walking (Martian) tripod** would be a lovely thing to see. No heat rays, though!"

—*Doktor A*

"I'd like to see someone build a dirigible: **a real, functional Steampunk-style dirigible . . .**"

—*Herr Döktor*

"I would like to see Yoko Ono do a retro-futurism/Steampunk piece. I think she would have a pretty interesting take on it."

—*Louise Kiner*

"I would love to see Frank Miller do some Steampunk influenced story or artwork. . . . I can already picture beautifully contrasted black-and-white ink paintings with white smoke and black stylized gears, all done with that *Sin City* ruggedness and moodiness."

—*James Ng*

"I'd love to see the director Carl Rinsch make an adaptation of one of China Miéville's stories."

—*Keith Thompson*

"More Steampunk drones."

—*Danny Warner*

PUSHKAGRAD

From Designers and Fashionistas

"If I had the time and the necessary resources, I would **build my own vision of Captain Nemo's** *Nautilus*. This a crazy and huge project, but also a utopian one."
—*Maurice Grunbaum*

"I would like to see the Netherlands artist Jos de Vink **create one of his magnificent Stirling engines as large as a two-story house.** Made entirely of gleaming silicon bronze (the king of metals), it would literally last forever. Thermal heating could provide the energy source. Finally, it could be tied into an immense astronomical clock. As a piece of kinetic art, I believe it would have no rival."
—*Art Donovan*

"I would love to have **thousands of Liquid Lights** be the backdrop for David Bowie performing 'Space Oddity.'"
—*Tanya Clarke*

"I'd love to **design and build an entire pub/smoking lounge in my aesthetic.** Or a library . . ."
—*J. W. Kinsey*

"I really want **to assemble a group of alternate-history builders** who'd like to work on a team of Steampunk street puppets or life-sized marionettes. I think this would be a fun challenge artistically, theatrically, and mechanically. It would be cool to provide each builder with the same basic frame (size, dimension), but leave the aesthetics, mechanics, and backstory to the individual crafter. Once the puppets are all constructed, the group could create a story or play to incorporate them all. That's not so pie-in-the-sky, really. I think I'm gonna make a few calls. . . ." —*Paige Gardner Smith*

"I'd love to see the incredible horologist Eric Freitas build **a giant mechanical clock** that would fill the entire surface of a very large ceiling—complete with spotlights to cast moving shadows on the floor." —*Tanya Clarke*

"I discovered Paul Guinan and Anina Bennett's book *Boilerplate: History's Mechanical Marvel* while vending at a convention called SalonCon several years ago. I was completely taken by the realism in which the main character, a robot called Boilerplate, was portrayed illustratively, and seamlessly inserted into historical Victorian photographs. **I would love to see Boilerplate brought to life in full size and in full-metal accuracy.**" —*Karen von Oppen*

"I'd love to see **a Steampunk retrofit on a big boat.** Like a yacht or paddle wheel. Maybe this has already been done and I've missed it. But if not . . . Ahoy! Someone, get on this." —*Paige Gardner Smith*

ABOVE
Thomas Willeford. Photo by Francesca Myman.
LEFT
Steampunk Bird Hybrid by Paige Gardner Smith. Photo by Dim Horizon Studio.

From Storytellers

"There are too many to count, but one I hope to actually bring about in the near future is **a story published in the form of a deck of cards that gets shuffled each time it's read.**"
—*Jedediah Berry*

"**I started some of the research for an alternate-history Steampunk novel in which Toussaint L'Ouverture was not starved to death by the French when they tricked him into showing up for negotiations.** This creates a Haiti where Toussaint, who was mixed race, charts a different course than Dessalines. Where the Montgolfier family moves to the first free black Western republic and develops airships, and Haiti (one of the largest economies in the area; Napoleon traded away the entire Louisiana Purchase for the promise of help reinvading Haiti—it was that valuable—thus changing U.S. history) becomes a powerhouse of the Caribbean due to its airship force. And as the U.S. Civil War approaches, Haiti, England, and France have to decide what sides to take, risking a world war."
—*Tobias Buckell*

BELOW
Notes from a Time Traveler's Journal by Mandem

"I've realized recently that I've written over a *thousand pages*—about giant lizards from outer space. I don't know how I feel about that! I'm very

interested at the moment in retro-futurism in the sense of 1950s American science fiction, not necessarily Victorian-ish, so I might do something with that. **But K. W. Jeter said recently, how there's never been, cinematically at least, the visual equivalence of** *Blade Runner* **to Steampunk. That comment's stayed with me. It would be a fascinating thing to try. Though I have no idea how!"**

—*Lavie Tidhar*

"**First, the ultimate. If I had vast resources and sufficient time, I would create a living Steampunk experience: a neo-Victorian, stylish, self-sustainable compound. In which the life Steamtastic, both Indian and British, is lived 24-7, incorporating DIY projects, fully functional steam engines, art installations, and immersive audience participation events and conventions.** Like a living history venue but completely dedicated to Steampunk. Dress code mandatory. Ideally this place would be in grounds that had space for an Indian temple and for other groups of makers and visionaries to come and stay and add their tuppence ha'pennyworth, space for wandering aeronauts and intrepid bandits; not to mention a lake big enough for a working submarine and an animatronic giant squid. A girl can dream . . ."

—*Suna Dasi*

"**I have a group of characters (and associated fantasy world) that began when I was twelve as pretend games I played with my sister.** Over twenty years, I've filled countless sketchbooks, notebooks, and computer files with their exploits. I'd love to find a way to tell the story and do it justice, but at that point it becomes so big and detailed that even though I took a small part of it and managed to write a novel that I think is pretty good, when I mention it to anyone, it still feels embarrassing, like I was invited over to someone's house for lunch and brought seven suitcases of stuff with me."

—*Jaclyn Dolamore*

"**I would like for Tom Waits to narrate an audiobook recording of** *Dr. Seuss's Sleep Book*."

—*Jedediah Berry*

"**I'd love to see a brilliantly written, funny, high-production-value Steampunk movie come out of Hollywood. Something charming, whimsical, and honest to the genre that doesn't take itself too seriously. Something similar to the way** Clue **tackles the cozy mystery genre, or** Firefly **handles the space opera western. Possibly with a romantic element.**"

—*Gail Carriger*

"**I think the Cthulhu mythos is possibly well overdue for being made into an epic Hollywood film,** and not a modern reimagining of the works of Lovecraft, but instead one rooted in the world he really knew."

—*Kit Cox*

"Can Neill Blomkamp or Duncan Jones adapt my novel *Warchild* for a feature film? Or better yet, develop it à la the reboot of *Battlestar Galactica* for Syfy so it's not limited to a two-hour narrative. Let nobody say I don't dream big."

—*Karin Lowachee*

"I'd like to see Dan Chaon do high fantasy (*Game of Thrones*–style), I'd like to see Murakami do some sort of heist, *Ocean's Eleven*–type book, and I'd like everyone who worked on *Pushing Daisies* to make it come back for several more seasons."

—*Lev Rosen*

From Musicians and Performers

"I really want to do another performance art piece/story and take it to the next level of having fire dancing, silk aerials, acrobats, and other choreography in a much bigger space than what I've previously worked with—like a mini Cirque du Soleil." —*Crystal Bright*

"*The Asylum for Wayward Victorian Girls,* the movie. And it *will* happen. In another reality, it already has." —*Emilie Autumn*

"A Steampunk Bollywood musical. Definitely. If anyone out there wants to give us a wedge of cash to write that, we'd be happy." —*Sunday Driver*

"The pie that I'm baking right now is a participatory musical about a techno-utopian space colony. It is a theater piece which is also a giant multiplayer narrative game." —*The Lisps*

"We'd love to gear up a bit more and incorporate larger aesthetic components into our live shows, like a life-sized Mechanical Turk or a skyline of a burning Paris with geared zeppelin zip lines. . . . We'd also like to do a high-powered music video for our song 'Oscar Wilde, Super-Spy,' replete with motorized-velocipede chases, sword-cane battles atop dirigibles, and fiendish death rays." —*Bad September*

"I'd really like to see someone make an epic series of films based on the Godhead Trilogy by James Morrow: *Towing Jehova, Blameless in Abaddon,* and *The Eternal Footman.*"
　　　　　　　　　　　　　　　　　　—*Matt Dallow, Amour Obscur*

"Live theater with music of Clark Ashton Smith's *The Empire of the Necromancers.*"
　　　　　　　　　　　　　　　　　　—*Shelby Cinca, The Cassettes*

"A permanent international Steampunk museum would be good, showcasing and archiving the work of the best creators around the globe."
　　　　　　　　　　　　—*The Men That Will Not Be Blamed for Nothing*

"Does Guillermo del Toro finally making *At the Mountains of Madness* count?"
—*Richard, Unextraordinary Gentlemen*

"I don't think we've really heard any 'Steampunk' music, especially when it comes to instruments and how they have been recorded. . . . I'd love to work on a project that would involve tools from the age before the first studios. Taking the knowledge we have and developing an alternate-reality Victorian studio. For example, wire-recording was invented already in the 1890s. If we bend the rules a little, we could have vacuum-tube technology (first amplifier invented in 1906). With amplification, the possibilities would be endless, both with studio tools and with instruments."
—*James Spectrum, Pepe Deluxé*

Desirina Boskovich's short fiction has been published in *Clarkesworld*, *Fantasy Magazine*, *Realms of Fantasy*, *Lightspeed*, *Nightmare*, *Kaleidotrope*, *PodCastle*, *Drabblecast*, and anthologies such as *The Way of the Wizard*, *Aliens: Recent Encounters*, and *The Apocalypse Triptych*. Her nonfiction pieces on music, literature, and culture have appeared in *Lightspeed*, Weird Fiction Review, *Wonderbook*, and *The Steampunk Bible*. She is also the editor of *It Came From the North: An Anthology of Finnish Speculative Fiction* (Cheeky Frawg, 2013). By day, she works as a freelance copywriter and communications consultant. She lives in Atlanta with her partner and two dogs.

Jeff VanderMeer's most recent novels are *Annihilation*, *Authority*, and *Acceptance* from Farrar, Straus and Giroux. Paramount Pictures has acquired the movie rights. His critically acclaimed *Wonderbook* (Abrams Image) has been nominated for several awards. A three-time World Fantasy Award winner, VanderMeer has been a finalist for the Nebula, Philip K. Dick, and Shirley Jackson Awards, among others. His nonfiction appears in the *New York Times Book Review*, the *Guardian*, the *Washington Post*, and the *Los Angeles Times*. VanderMeer also serves as the co-director of Shared Worlds, a unique teen SF/fantasy writing camp located at Wofford College. Previous nonfiction titles include *Booklife* and *The Steampunk Bible*. He lives in Tallahassee, Florida, with his wife, the noted editor Ann VanderMeer.

ACKNOWLEDGMENTS

Our very heartfelt thanks to our editor, David Cashion. His thoughtful advice helped improve this manuscript immensely and his gentle nudging helped keep the process on track. Thanks also to managing editors Lauren Hougen and David Blatty, and to designer Darilyn Carnes, who did such a fantastic job transforming our vision into a book—we couldn't be happier. And thank you as well to agent Sally Harding.

Huge thanks also go to Adam Mills, whose tireless assistance on conducting interviews and acquiring images was absolutely essential to the book, as well as to the infinitely patient Ann VanderMeer, who took time out of her own busy schedule to provide a great deal of administrative and organizational support. And, thank you as well to S. J. Chambers, whose initial brainstorming and research helped launch the project.

Many, many people contributed their talents to this book, and we are deeply grateful to them all. Many contributors went above and beyond, working under short deadlines, offering even more than we had asked, and coming up with fantastic ideas of their own. For example, Thomas Willeford, who swooped in to save the day with the fantastic mecha-penguin featured in Chapter One. We're also immensely grateful to Jess Nevins, John Coulthart, and Jake von Slatt, along with William Francis, Adrian Van Allen, and Matt Lorenz. Furthermore, this book would not exist without the wonderful contributions of James MacIntyre, Toni Green, Catherine Cheek, Ramona Szczerba, Molly Crabapple, Katherine Gleason, Bruce and Melanie Rosenbaum, Megan Maude, Richard Preston, Jeremy Zerfoss, Ivica Stevanovic, Irene Gallo, Matthew Cheney, Diana M. Pho, Eric Farber, and Nancy Hightower. And, additional thanks go to Jason Heller, Will Hindmarch, and Carrie Vaughn.

Finally, an extremely sincere thank-you to everyone who agreed to be interviewed for this manual and granted permission for us to reprint images of their work. Your creativity and expertise are the cornerstone of this book.

All images with copyright © 2014 created exclusively for the Steampunk User's Manual. All sidebar articles and project descriptions were created exclusively for this book and are copyright © 2014 to the creators indicated by their byline. All images in this book are under copyright and cannot be reused without express permission of the copyright holders.

Cover: (left) © 2014 Thomas Willeford, (center) © 2011 John Mondelli, (right) © 2009 Guy Himber aka V&A Steamworks

Interior: **2–3**: © 2012 Guy Himber aka V&A Steamworks; **4**: © 2012 James Ng; **7**: © 2010 Sam Van Olffen; **8–9**: © 2013 Thomas Willeford; **10–11**: © 2013 Sam Van Olffen; **13**: © 2012 Ria Osborne; **14**: © 2011 Third Rail Projects, LLC; **15**: (top) © 2013 Matt Lorenz, (bottom) © 2014 Oscar Sanmartin Vargas; **16**: © 2013 Joseph O'Connell and Blessing Hancock; **18**: Because We Can © 2013 Jon Sarriugarte & Kyrsten Mate; **19**: © 2011 Third Rail Projects, LLC; **20–21**: © 2011 Keith Thompson ("Peace Treaty interior illustration reprinted with the permission of Simon Pulse, an imprint of Simon & Schuster Children's Publishing Division from The Manual of Aeronautics: An Illustrated Guide to the Leviathan Series by Scott Westerfeld illustrated by Keith Thompson."); **24**: © 2012 Daniel Warner; **25**: © 2012 Bruce Whistlecraft; **26, 27**: copyright © 2013 Henrietta's Eye (Libby Bulloff and Stephen Robinson); **28**: © 2012 Brian Kesinger; **29**: (top) © 2014 Mike Pecci, (bottom) © 2010 Jake von Slatt; **30, 31, 32, 33**: © 2013 Nathan Sorochan; **35**: © 2012 Thomas Willeford; **36, 37**: © Paul St George 2008; **38**: © 2013 James Ng; **40**: © 2009 Keith Thompson; **41**: © 2013 Oscar Sanmartin Vargas; **42**: (top) © 2009 Annliz Bonin/anXiogène, (bottom) © 2013 Bruce Whistlecraft; **43**: © 2004 Paul Harvey; **44, 45, 46, 47**: © 2014 Catherine Cheek; **48**: © 2009 Louise Kiner; **49**: © 2010 Louise Kiner; **51**: © 2013 Carrie Ann Baade; **52–53**: © 2013 Carrie Ann Baade; **55**: © 2010 Jake von Slatt; **56, 57, 58, 59**: Images © 2013 and text © 2014 William Francis and Adrian Van Allen; **60**: © 2008 Guy Himber aka V&A Steamworks; **61**: © 2014 Mauricio A. Cordero, with Nautilus project created for **5** Wits Entertainment by Joey Marsocci (copyright © 2013) with assistants Steve Ziolkowski and Brendan Wilson; **62–63**: © 2013 Ramona Szczerba; **64**: © 2014 Desirina Boskovich; **66, 67**: © 2014 Ramona Szczerba; **68–69**: © 2006 Pierre Matter; **68**: © 2003 Pierre Matter; **71**: © 2008 Guy Himber aka V&A Steamworks; **72**: © 2000 Oscar Sanmartin Vargas; **73**: © 2008 Pierre Matter; **74–75, 77, 79, 81**: Images © 2014 Thomas Willeford; **76**: © 2013 Ken Swallow; **82–83**: Illustration © 2014 John Coulthart; **84**: © 2012 Tas Limur; **86**: © 2013 Michael Hansmeyer; **87, 88**: © 2013 Joel Aron Photography; **89**: © 2010 Amanda Scrivener; **90**: © 2010 Amanda Scrivener; **91**: © 2014 Molly Crabapple; **93**: © 2013 Meredith Zinner Photography; **94**: © 2013 Meredith Zinner Photography; **95**: © 2013 Meredith Zinner Photography; **96**: © 2013 Joshua W. Kinsey; **97**: © 2009, © 2010 Tanya Clarke; **98**: © 2013 Art Donovan; **100, 101**: © 2007 Because We Can; **102–103**: © David Donde; **104–105**: © Shanna Jones; **106** (top): © Shanna Jones, (bottom) © David Donde; **107**: © 2008 Andy Jordan; **108**: (top) © 2010 Kyle Cassidy, (bottom) © 2012 Dim Horizon Studios; **109**: © 2013 Art Attack Films; **110**: © 2012 Maurice Grunbaum; **111**: © 2013 Dim Horizon Studios; **112**: © 2013 Joseph O'Connell and Blessing Hancock; **113**: © 2013 J. W. Kinsey; **114**: © 2010 Amanda Scrivener; **115**: © 2013 Michele LoBosco Photography; **116**: © 2013 Art Attack Films; **117**: © 2013 Michael Hansmeyer; **118–119**: © Jon Sarriugarte & Kyrsten Mate; **125**: © 2004 Paul Harvey; **126**: © 2012 Deborah Selwood/Gecko Studios Photography Limited; **127**: © 2009 Art Donovan; **128**: © 2009 Tas Limur; **136–137**: Illustration © 2014 John Coulthart; **138**: © 2011 Angry Robot Books; **142**: (top) © 2012 Barry Rosenthal, (bottom) © 2011 Stephanie J. Boland; **143**: (top) © 2012 Lucy Hamblin, (bottom) © 2009 Penguin Press; **144–145**: © 2005 John Picacio; **146**: (top) © 2011 Caren Ann Corley, (bottom) © 2013 Henry Faber; **147**: (top) © 2013 ActuSF, (bottom) © 2013 Étienne Barillier and Arthur Morgan; **149**: © 2001 John Coulthart; **150–151**: © 2013 Pavel Trávníček; **152**: (top) © 2006 Tor Books, (bottom) © Ivson Miranda/Itaú Cultural; **153**: © 2010 Angry Robot Books; **154–155**: © 2014 Jeremy Zerfoss; **156**: © 2011 Jennifer and J. K. Potter; **157**: (top) © 2013 Nadya Kwandibens/ Red Works Photography, (bottom) © 2011 HarperCollins; **158**: © 2011 Jake von Slatt; **159**: © 2011 Jake von Slatt; **161**: © 2013 Angry Robot Books; **162–163**: © 2013 John Jennings; **164**: (left) © 2012 Tachyon, (right) © 2013 Scarecrow Press; **165**: © 2014 Jeremy Zerfoss based on concepts by Will Hindmarch; **166**: © 2012 Tor Books; **167**: (top) © 2010 Jon Foster, (bottom) © 2013 Tor Books; **168**: © 2011 Tor Books; **169**: (top) © 2009 Benjamin Carré, (bottom) © 2009 David Malki !; **170**: © 2014 Ivica Stevanovic; **171**: © 2013 Dade W. Bell; **172**: (top) © 2008 Larissa Johnson, (bottom) © 2009 Jamie Nygaard; **173**: © 2009 Guy Himber aka V&A Steamworks; **174**: © 2006 James A. Owen; **178–179**: © 2014 Ivica Stevanovic; **180–181**: Illustration © 2014 John Coulthart; **182**: © 2008 David S. Holloway; **184**: © 2013 SteamFunk Productions, LLC; **185**: (top) © 2007 Sid Penance, (bottom) © 2013 Unextraordinary Gentlemen; **187**: © 2013 Bonnie Stanley; **189**: © 2012 Evgenia Eliseeva; **190, 191**: © 2012 Jan Jefferies; **192**: (top) © 2012 Paul Shapera, (bottom) © 2012 Paul Shapera; **193, 194, 195**: © photographer Enrique Carnicero and Tribe Theatre; **196**: © 2013 Rachael Shane **197**: © 2013 LoS Productions LLC; **198**: © 2012 Miriam Rosenburg Roček; **199**: © 2013 Rachael Shane; **200**: © 2011 Voltaire; **201**: © 2013 Voltaire; **202**: © 2008 Abney Park; **203**: © 2011 Lex Machina; **204**: © 2012 Ria Osborne; **205**: © 2011 Melissa King; **207**: (top) © 2012 Paul Alborough & Tom Caruana; (bottom) © 2012 Ele Grievson/Curious Magpie Photography; **208, 209, 211**: © 2013 Dani Leventhal; **212, 213, 215, 216, 217**: © 2014 Matt Lorenz; **218–219**: © 2013 Tod Seelie; **220**: © 2012 Daniella Koontz; **222**: © 2012 Daniella Koontz; **223**: © 2008 Greg Nomoora; **224**: © 2011 Third Rail Projects, LLC; **225**: © 2011 Third Rail Projects, LLC; **226**: (top) copyright © 2014 Ediciones Nevsky; **226, 227, 228, 229**: © 2013 Charlotte Frantzdatter/Frantzdatter Photography; **231**: © 2012 Jonathan Doyle/jjdoyle.com; **232**: © 2010 Carrie Ann Baade; **234**: © 2012 Annliz Bonin/anXiogène; **235**: © 2012 John Coulthart; **236**: © 2010 Ramona Szczerba; **237**: © 2008 James Ng; **238–239**: © 2013 Jon Sarriugarte & Kyrsten Mate; **240**: © 2006 Keith Thompson; **241**: (top) © 2012 Francesca Myman, (bottom) © 2013 Dim Horizon Studios; **243**: © 2013 Mark Cordory; **244**: (top) © 2011 Third Rail Projects, LLC (Tom Pearson), (bottom) © 2011 John Mondelli; **245**: © 2013 Bonnie Stanley; **246**: © 2008 Carrie Ann Baade; **247**: (top) © 2012 Jonathan Doyle/jjdoyle.com, (bottom) The Men That Will Not Be Blamed For Nothing copyright © 2013 Martin SoulStealer; **248–249**: © 2014 Daniel Warner; **250**: (top) © 2012 Joshua Campbell, (bottom) © Francesca Myman/Locus Publications; **256**: © 2013 Charlotte Frantzdatter/Frantzdatter Photography.

Design icons: **5, 6, 30, 42, 44, 56, 64, 74, 92, 114, 120, 130, 166, 176, 190, 196, 206, 208, 212, 226**; and design patterns: **23, 85, 139, 183, 233**, and endpapers by Heesang Lee.

INDEX

Page numbers in *italic* refer to illustrations and photographs.

Abney Park, 202, *202*, 222
Absinthe Drinkers, 189, 204
Adams, John Joseph, 167, *167*
The Afterlife of the Honeybees (Baade), *232*, 234
The Airship "Mary Chickering" (Kiner), *49*
Airship Smuggler (Dasi), *116*
All Men of Genius (Rosen; McKowen art), 168, *168*
Alvarez, César, 188, 208, 218, 220
Amour Obscur, 218–219, *218–219*, 221, 246
The Amperial Orrery (Kinsey), *96*
Anders, Charlie Jane, 160
Anderson, Jill, *93*, 94, 95, *95*
Archangel (Costa), *107*
Astigmatismo divino (Sanmartín Vargas), *41*
Astonish! (Hindmarch; Zerfoss art), *165*
The Asylum for Wayward Victorian Girls (Autumn), 225
Autumn, Emilie, 188–189, *205*, 224–225, 245
Ayeni, Yomi, 198

Baade, Carrie Ann, 50–51, *51*, *52–53*, *54*, 70, 234, *246*
Bacigalupi, Paolo, 148
Bad September, 245
Ballroom Luminoso (O'Connell and Hancock), *16*, *112*
Barcia, Jacques, 141, 143, 152, *152*, 174
Barillier, Étienne, *147*, 148
Bassington Brain (von Slatt), 159, *159*
Batterie-en-Valise (Farber), *209*
"Beatrice" (Tidbeck), 195, 226–229, *227*, *228*, *229*
Bennett, Felix, *36*
Berry, Jedediah, 143, *143*, 171, 175, 242, 243
Binoculares de compañía (Sanmartín Vargas), *41*

bonebox, 212–213, *212*, *213*
Bonin, Annliz, *42*, 49, 234, *234*, 236
The Bookman (Tidhar; Frankland cover), 153, *153*
The Bookman Histories (Tidhar; Coulthart cover), *161*
bottle cap magnets, 44–47
The Bride Stripping the Bachelors Bare (Baade), *246*
Bright, Crystal, 186, *187*, 200, 204, *245*
Broaddus, Maurice, 146, 172, *172*
Buckell, Tobias, 141, 152, *152*, 172–173, *172*, 242
Bulloff, Libby, 25–27, *26*, *27*, 35, 42, 49, 60, 73
Busk, Andreas, 227–228

Camera Obscura (Tidhar), *138*
canjo, 214–217, *215*, *216*, *217*
Carena, Elisabeth, *225*, *244*
Carriger, Gail, 243
The Cassettes, *182*, 200, 204, 205, 246
Cederstrand, Sarah Piyannah, 227–228
Chai Cycle (MacIntyre), *30*, 31–32, *31*, *32*, *33*
chair back with cans (Lorenz), *15*
Cheek, Catherine, 44–47
Chen, Anna, 141, 170, 190–191, *190*
Cheney, Matthew, 176–177
Chronoclasmic Inhibitor (von Slatt), 158–159, *158*
Cinca, Shelby, 223
Clarke, Tanya, 97, *97*, 126–127, 129, 240, 241
Clock (Bonin), *42*
Clockwork Dolls, 202–203
The Cog is Dead, *220*, 222, *244*
Cordory, Mark, 34–35, *73*, *126*, *243*
Costa, Kristin, *107*, 108, 114, 116, 118, 126
Coulthart, John, *149*, *161*, *235*
Cox, Kit, 243
Crabapple, Molly, *91*
Crossland, Samantha R., 95
Crystal Rain (Buckell; Lockwood cover), *152*

Curval, Allison, 221
Cyberlove (Matter), *68*

Dadd, Richard, 180–181
Dark Garden Corsetry, *87*, *88*
Dasi, Suna, *109*, *116*, 146–147, *146*, 153, 156, 171, 173, 243
Davis, Milton, 164–165
Death on the Nile (Willis; Maronski cover), *141*
Detroit Installation (Wagner), 82–83
Digital Grotesque (Hansmeyer and Dillenburger), *86*, 117
Dillenburger, Benjamin, *86*, 117
Diorama 3 (Sanmartín Vargas), *72*
DIY approach, 48–51, 116–117, 156–157, 205
Doktor A, 14, 25–27, *25*, *26*, 35, 42, *42*, 49, 60–61, 70, 73, 234, 236
Dolamore, Jaclyn, 143, 150, *171*, 172, 243
The Dolls of New Albion (Shapera), 192, *192*, 194
album cover by de Korte, 192, *192*
motion poster by Warner, 24, *24*
Dolly Pheasant Hunter Spats (Scrivener), *90*
Donovan, Art, 96–97, *98*, 99, 112, 114, 117, 119, 127, *127*, 129, 240
Dradin, In Love (VanderMeer), *193*, 194–195, *194*, *195*
Dreamkeeper, Olivier, *110*
Drozdov, Andrey, 25–27, *26*, 35, 42, 49, 60
Ducha de portátil (Portable Shower) (Sanmartín Vargas), *41*

El-Mohtar, Amal, 142, *142*
The Encyclopedia of Fantastic Victoriana (Nevins; Picacio cover), *144–145*
"Exorcist" (Ng), *4*
Extremes of Retrofuturist Inspiration (Stevanovic), *170*

Falksen, G. D., 168, *169*
Farber, Eric, 208–211, *208*, *209*, *211*

flamingo sculpture (Joslin), *54*
Flotilla (Szczerba), *62–63*
found-percussion, 208–211, *208, 209, 211*
Foundry Theatre, 210, 211
Francis, William, 56–59, *56, 57, 58, 59*
Futurity, 189

Gilman, Felix, 166, *166, 167*
Givens, Mark, 14
Gleason, Katherine, 92–95
Gothic Dead Faery Skeleton Mini Top Hat (Scrivener), *114*
The Grand Master (Donovan), *98*
The Great Mechanical Unicorn (Van Olffen), *10–11*
The Great Steam Colossus, Sphen 1 (Willeford), 74–81, *74–75, 77, 81*
Green, Toni, 32
Grunbaum, Maurice, *110*, 111, 240
Grymm, Dr., *61*
Le Guide Steampunk (Barillier and Morgan), *147*
Gunn, Eileen, 168, *169*
Gupta, Savan, *184*

Hancock, Blessing, *16, 112*
Hansmeyer, Michael, *86, 117*
Harvester (Ng), *237*
Harvey, Paul, 42, *43, 125*
Heintz, Andy, 203, *204*
Here, There Be Dragons (Owen), *174*
Herr Döktor, 12, 25–27, *26,* 34, 35, 42, 49, 60, 70, 72, 236
Hewitt, Jema, 90, 115, 116, 126, 129
Hiding (Kesinger), 27, *28*
Hightower, Nancy, 226–229, *226, 227, 228, 229*
Himber, Guy, *2–3, 60,* 70, *71, 173*
Hindmarch, Will, *165*
Hommage Ö Ader (Matter), *73*

I'm British (Professor Elemental), *188, 207*
Industrial Revolution (Coulthart), *235*
Italian Widow Dress (Anderson), *94, 95*

Jagannath (Tidbeck; Ramón cover art), *226*

Joslin, Jessica, *54*
Journal 1878 (Kiner), *48*
Julie (Bonin), *234*

Kesinger, Brian, 27, *28*
Killjoy, Magpie, 60
Kiner, Louise, 43, *48,* 49–50, *49,* 61, 70, 72–73, 234, 237
Kinsey, J. W., *96, 113,* 240
Kraken vs. Airship (Preston; Zerfoss cover), *154–155*

LaPensée, Elizabeth, *157*
The League of S.T.E.A.M., 197–198, *197*
"Lightbringers and Rainmakers" (Gilman; Foster art), 166, *167*
Lilies on Stage (Doktor A), *25*
"Liquid Light" (Clarke), *97*
Lisps, 188, *189,* 210, 218, 245
London–New York Telectroscope (St George), *86*
Lorenz, Matt, 212–217, *212, 213, 215, 216, 217*
Lowachee, Karin, 175, 244

MacIntyre, James, *30,* 31–33, *31, 32, 33*
The Mad King and His Odd Airships (Stevanovic), *178–179*
The Mad Scientist's Guide to World Domination (Adams; Templesmith art), 166, *166*
magnets, bottle cap, 44–47
Mandem, *242*
The Manual of Aeronautics (Westerfeld; Thompson art), *20–21*
The Manual of Detection (Berry), 143, *143*
Maronski, Tomasz, *141*
Martin, Haldane, 102–106, *102–103, 104–105, 106*
Mate, Kyrsten, *19, 118–119, 238–239*
Matter, Pierre, 68, *68, 69, 73*
Maude, Megan, 120–124, *120*
McGrew, Jeffrey, 100–101, *100, 101*
McQueen, Lee Alexander, 92–95
The Mechanisms, *207*
Mecha-penguin (Willeford), 74–81, *74–75, 77, 79, 81*
Mecha-spider (Willeford), *35*

The Men That Will Not Be Blamed for Nothing, 203–204, *203, 204,* 205, 246, *247*
Miller, Scott, 74–81
ModVic, 118
Mollusc Tree (Thompson), *39*
Mondelli, John, *220*
Morgan, Arthur, 147–148, *147*
Morin, Rebekah, *14*
Mothership (Campbell and Hall; Jennings cover), *162–163*

Nath, Chandy, *247*
Nautilus (Dr. Grymm), *61*
Nevins, Jess, 136–137
Newitz, Annalee, 160
Ng, James, *4, 34, 38, 39,* 61, 68–69, 236, 237, *237*
Northrup, Jillian, 100–101, *100, 101*
Notes from a Time Traveler's Journal (Mandem), *242*

O'Connell, Joe, *16, 112*
Ojetade, Balogun, 165
Omnia Vanitas (Bulloff and Robinson), *26*
O'Neill, Andrew, *13*
Orrery (Francis and Van Allen), 56–59, *56, 57, 58, 59*
Owen, James A., *174,* 175

Palabres (Matter), *69*
Peace Treaty (Thompson), *20–21*
Pecci, Mike, *29*
The Penguin (Swallow), *76*
Pennsylvania (Farber), *211*
Pepe Deluxé, *247*
Pho, Diana, 143, 150, 170, 175, 196–199, *196, 199*
Picacio, John, *144–145*
Plnou Parou (Šust; Trávníček cover), *150–151,* 164
Portrait of Harlan Glotzer (Bulloff and Robinson), *26*
Potter, Jennifer and J. K., *156*
Prague (Praha) (Van Olffen), *7*
Preston, Richard E., Jr., 148, 150–151, *154–155,* 171
Punk Victorian (Harvey), *125*
Pushkagrad (Thompson), *240*

Queen of Swords (Szczerba), *236*
Queen of the Wave (Pepe Deluxé), 192

Racoon Express (Ng), *38*
Reade House, 136–137
The Red Oak Suitcase (collapsed) (Farber), *208*
A Reel-to-Reel Recording Machine (Kinsey), *113*
The Rise of Ransom City (Gilman; MacDonald art), 166, *166*
The Road to Atlantis (Grunbaum and Dreamkeeper), *110*
Robinson, Stephen, 25–27, *26, 27*
Rococopunk Jacket (Maude), 120–124, *120*
Roček, Miriam Rosenberg, 197, 198–199, *198*
Rosen, Lev, 142, *142*, 151–152, 168, *168*, 175, 244
Rosenbaum, Bruce, 99, 113, 115, 127, 129, 130–135
Rosenbaum, Melanie, 130–135
Rowell, Jessica, *84*, 115, *115*, 116, 125, 126–127, *128*, 129

samovar, Turkish brass, 31, *31*
Sanmartín Vargas, Oscar, *15, 41, 72*
Sarriugarte, Jon, *19, 118–119, 238–239*
Scotolati, Eric, *108*
Scrivener, Amanda, 89–90, *89, 90, 114*, 115
Serpent Twins (Sarriugarte and Mate), *19*, 118, *118–119, 238–239*
Shapera, Paul, 192, *192*, 194
Shawl, Nisi, 146, *146*, 153
HMS *Shelman* (Himber), *60*
Shiva Mandala (Donovan), *127*
Shutterburg (Doktor A), *42*
Smith, Paige Gardner, 89, 107–109, *108*, 111, *111*, 115, 117, 125–126, 129, 241, *241*
Snakes and Ladders (Coulthart), *149*
stand-up greeting, collaged, 64–67
Stanley, Justin, 197
Stars Pulled Down (Unextraordinary Gentlemen; Pilawski art), *185*
Steamarama house, 130–135
Steam Atlantis (Grunbaum), *110*
Steamfunk (Davis), 164–165
Steaming into a Victorian Future (Taddeo and Miller; Watson cover), *164*

Steammpunk III: Steampunk Revolution (VanderMeer; Story cover), *164*
Steampunk Bird Hybrid (Smith), *241*
Steampunk bus (von Slatt), *29*
Steampunk DevaDasis (Dasi), *109*
Steampunk Haunted House (Morris and Third Rail Projects), *18*
Steampunk III: Steampunk Revolution (VanderMeer; Story cover art), *164*
Steampunk Magazine, 41
The Steampunk Opium Wars (Chen), 190–191, *190, 191*
Stevanovic, Ivica, *170, 178–179*
St George, Paul, 36, *36, 37*, 43, 73, 236
"The Strange Case of Mr. Salad Monday" (Falksen; Malki art), 168, *169*
The Stuckists Punk Victorian (Harvey), *43*
Sunday Driver, 201, 221, 222, *231*, 245, *247*
Surface King (Thompson), *40*
Swallow, Ken, *76*
Swanwick, Michael, 168, *169*
Szczerba, Ramona, 12, 43, *62–63, 64–67, 64, 66, 67, 236, 236*

Tamara (Rowell), *115*
Teeth (Bulloff and Robinson), *26, 27*
Telectroscope (St George), 36, *36, 37*
Teléfono de campaña (Sanmartín Vargas), *41*
Tempest (Warner), *248–249*
"TESLA Man; Machine" (Himber), *71*
La Tetera de Hobart (Hobart's Kettle) (Sanmartín), *15*
The Thackery T. Lambshead Cabinet of Curiosities (VanderMeer and VanderMeer), 157, *157*
Then She Fell, 14, 224, 225, *225*
Thompson, Keith, *20–21*, 39, *39, 40*, 73, 236, 237, *240*
Three Rings (McGrew and Northrup), 100–101, *100, 101*
Tidbeck, Karin, 195, 226–229, *226, 227*

Tidhar, Lavie, *138*, 153, *153, 161*, 175, 242–243
Tidsrum, 227–229, *227, 228, 229*
Tjalve, Ida Marie, 227, 229
Tornado Jane (Smith), *108*
Townsend-Pehlke, Morrigana, 115, 117, 129
Trávníček, Pavel, *150–151*
Truth Coffee (Martin), 102–106, *102–103, 104–105, 106*
Tunis, Sammy, *189*

ukelele, embellished, *244*
Unextraordinary Gentlemen, 184, *185*, 186, 247
Utopian Flying Machines of the Previous Century (from The Dream of Flight), *22*

Van Allen, Adrian, 56–59, *56, 57, 58, 59*
VanderMeer, Ann, 142, 146, 157, *157, 164*
VanderMeer, Jeff, 143, 146, 157, *157, 193*, 194–195, *194*
Van Olffen, Sam, *7, 10–11*, 43, 70
"Victorian Robo Detective and Dr. WATTson" (Himber), *2–3*
Viglione, Brian, 223, *223*
Viking Jacket (Anderson), *93*
Voltaire, 200, *200, 201*, 223
von Oppen, Karen, 241
von Slatt, Jake, 28, *29*, 39, *55*, 82–83, 157, 158–160, *158, 159, 160*
Von Slatt Steampunker (Pecci), *29*
Voyage (Himber), *173*

Wagner, Emily, 82–83
Ward, Carlton Cyrus, 224
Warner, Danny, 12, 24, *24*, 39, 41, 43, 70, 237, *248–249*
Willeford, Thomas, *8–9*, 35, *35*, 48–49, 74–81, *74–75, 77, 79, 80–81, 236, 241*
Wooden Bunny with Brass Wings (Scrivener), *89*

"Zeppelin City" (Gunn and Swanwick; Carre art), 168, *169*
Zoetica (Rowell), *128*

Editor: David Cashion
Designer: Darilyn Lowe Carnes
Cover Designer: Galen Smith
Production Manager: Denise LaCongo

Library of Congress Control Number: 2014930775

ISBN: 978-1-4197-0898-5

Printed and bound in the United States
10 9 8 7 6 5 4 3 2 1

Abrams Image books are available at special discounts when
purchased in quantity for premiums and promotions as well
as fundraising or educational use. Special editions can
also be created to specification. For details, contact
specialsales@abramsbooks.com or the address below.

THE ART OF BOOKS SINCE 1949

115 West 18th Street
New York, NY 10011
www.abramsbooks.com